Funny Side Up:

Dishing Out Dad's Advice

by Warren S. Murray

Son of legendary comedian Jan Murray

Written by
Warren S. Murray

Edited by Steve Schwab
Cover Art and Layout by Helane Freeman

Copyright © 2021 Warren S. Murray
All rights reserved.

Warren S. Murray
WAWA PUBLISHING
Moorpark, CA
warrensmurray@hotmail.com

For permission requests, sales to U.S. bookstores and
wholesalers, or to inquire about quantity discounts, please
contact the publisher at the email address above.

Printed in the United States of America
Library of Congress Control Number: 2021909431
ISBN – 978-0-9961516-6-5

First Edition
10 9 8 7 6 5 4 3 2 1

Funny Side Up:

Dishing Out Dad's Advice

To FRAN, my muse, my love, my everything.

TABLE OF CONTENTS

INTRODUCTION

Being the son of comedian Jan Murray gave me a unique point of view about every aspect of life. To illustrate, let me take you back to my youth. Dad had been out of town for a one week engagement, headlining the show at the famous Chez Paree nightclub in Chicago. When he returned, my family sat down to eat dinner and Dad asked me how my week had gone. It had gone badly. I had a big fight with my best friend, received a D on a math test at school, and my girlfriend broke up with me. I was angry and sad and my narrative was fueled by self-pity.

Dad listened sympathetically and then said: "Let's change places. You're me and I'm you. Now ask me how my week went."

I did and Dad retold my entire story back to me. This time, however, he embellished some points, added a few details and tweaked other parts of my tale of woe. The result was a hilarious recitation of my travails that sent the whole table, including me, into hysterical laughter.

I said, "That was great, but you really bent the truth in your version."

He waved his finger at me. "Do you want truth or laughs?"

I thought a bit and decided I wanted both.

Dad smiled, delighted with my answer. "Son" (he always called me that when he couldn't remember my name), "all comedy is based on truth. All you have to do is find what's humorous about it. Almost everything in life has a funny side to it – life, death, marriage, taxes, everything. All you have to do to get laughs is pick a topic and find the funny side of that topic."

As a comedian's son, I got to meet the apex of American standup comics in the middle and second half of the twentieth century. As a television comedy writer, and later as the head of NBC's comedy programming department, I met a "Who's Who" of stars, producers, directors and actors. In between, there were marriages, travel and adventures.

In this book, I will attempt to examine all the people, places and events I've experienced. This is not an autobiography, although each story was either witnessed by, overheard or actually happened to me. I guess that makes it a memoir-ish. My chapters are in alphabetical order, not chronological. All the stories are true, but, following Dad's admonition, they may be slightly modified so that when you read these accounts, you will hopefully experience not only the truth, but even better, you'll get them dished out to you FUNNY SIDE UP.

MILTON BERLE

"Uncle Miltie" was the first major star of a new technology called television. When his show, "Texaco Star Theater Starring Milton Berle" premiered, there were only a few thousand TV sets in the U.S. The show generated such enormous word-of-mouth acclaim, literally millions of people purchased TV sets just to see his show. It was so popular that people closed their stores and rushed home to see his program every Tuesday night. Within a few years, Berle became the biggest and highest-paid star in America.

Milton was close friends with my father. They played golf together, and Dad and Toni (my stepmother) often dined out or at each other's homes with Milton and his then-wife, Ruth Cosgrove. Berle, like George Burns, was never seen without a cigar. When he came to our house, Toni would follow him around with an ashtray as Milton was prone to flick his cigar ashes wherever he was sitting or standing.

He adored our family, and before all the New York Catskill comics moved to California, they were rabid Dodger, Giant or Yankee fans. When I was a child, Milton pulled up to Dad's house with a limo and drove us all to Ebbets Field to watch a World Series game between my beloved Bums and the hated New York Yankees. Milton treated us all to box seats behind home plate as we watched Brooklyn win the game.

When I was fourteen, my dad bought me golf lessons. After a while I became quite good and he let me play with him on various courses. One day he told me we were going to play a round of golf with Uncle Miltie. Dad wanted him to see how big I'd gotten and how well I played golf.

Soon after we arrived at the course, we were on the practice putting green when Milton spotted us and he shouted out:

"Hi, Jan. Hi, Warren." PFFFFT! He let out the loudest fart I'd ever heard in my young life.

My father grabbed my arm and pulled me aside. "Milton has an obstruction in his anal cavity," he explained to me in hushed tones, "and whenever he gets excited, he passes wind. He's having a procedure tomorrow, but he's very self-conscious about it. So make believe you don't notice."

Being an obnoxious teenager, I chirped, "How can I not notice? They heard it in Pittsburgh!"

"Don't be a smart-ass," Dad hissed. "Just don't say anything."

When we got to the first tee, word got out that Milton Berle and Jan Murray were about to tee off and a small crowd gathered. My father announced to them, "This is my son, Warren. He hits the ball like a gorilla. Show them what you've got, son."

I took my stance, brought my club back, and just as I started my transition forward, I heard PFFFT! I missed the ball completely! I turned to give Berle a piece of my mind, but Dad signaled me to be quiet and I reluctantly turned away.

For the next twelve holes, my game went to pieces as Milton loudly passed wind seemingly every time I attempted to strike the ball. Finally, on the 13th tee, Dad sliced his drive deep into the woods on the right and Berle went into the small bathroom that was set up behind the tee. Alone at last, I hit a towering drive to the center of the fairway. Milton emerged from the restroom and hit his drive about 30 yards shorter than my drive – but in the same exact direction.

So, as Dad disappeared into the woods to look for his ball, Milton put his arm around my shoulder and for the next 200-plus yards I had to listen to: "Warren, my boy, PFFFT, you sure have grown. PFFFT. Are you going into comedy like your father? PFFFT!"

By the time we reached his ball, I was shell-shocked from the loud, odorous explosions I had just endured. Milton turned to me and asked, "How far PFFFT do you think I am PFFFT to the flag? PFFFT."

I looked and saw my father was still in the woods. I turned back to Berle and said,

"Milton, I'd say you've got anywhere between 145 to 150 FARTS to the flag!"

When Dad emerged from the woods, he was astonished to see Milton Berle chasing after his son, trying to brain him with a 6-iron!

Through the years I saw Milton many times at the house and even played golf with him again. Neither of us ever mentioned the "fart incident" and he always treated me with a big smile and a hug. I was relieved that he had either forgiven me or had forgotten the occurrence completely.

Dinner with Milton, Dad, Toni, and my date, Linda Goldstein, at a nightclub in 1961

The last time I saw him was at the Friar's Club in Los Angeles, where they were honoring my father with a roast before inducting him into the Wall of Fame. This was a good twenty or more years after that crazy day on the golf course. Berle was in the audience, but couldn't perform because he was recovering from a stroke and could barely walk or talk. When he saw me, he managed to raise a finger and signal me to come to him. When I arrived, he beckoned me to bend down so he could whisper something in my ear. I put my ear close to his mouth and Mr. Television said, "PFFFFFFFFFFFT!"

Later in his life, Milton was the "Toastmaster General" for the Friar's Club, presiding over every testimonial dinner/roast they held for many years. Milton and just about all the comics he roasted are gone now, but I'm sure that he's up there somewhere, smoking his cigars, roasting his friends and blasting the sky with his heavenly farts.

GEORGE BURNS

George Burns was, and is still considered, an American treasure. Born in 1894, his career spanned vaudeville, radio, nightclubs, TV and movies. Playing straight man to his hilarious wife, Gracie Allen, George kind of disappeared from public awareness after her death. Then, in 1974, when he was 80, his best friend, Jack Benny, was diagnosed with pancreatic cancer and asked George to take over his role in an upcoming movie called "The Sunshine Boys." Burns won a Best Supporting Actor Oscar for his role, kickstarting a remarkable run of hits that ended only upon his death, at age 100.

On my father's 75th birthday, he held an elaborate party celebration at his home in Beverly Hills. All of Dad's show business buddies attended with their spouses. Buddy Hackett was there, along with Sid Caesar, Danny Thomas, Red Buttons, Morey Amsterdam, Norm Crosby, Milton Berle, Jerry Lewis, Totie Fields, Phyllis Diller, Don Rickles, and a host of actors and singers including Steve Lawrence, Eydie Gorme and Jerry Vale. But the biggest star there, the one who everyone gathered around to listen to his stories all evening, was George Burns.

One of the stories Burns regaled us with that night had to do with Jack Benny. It seems that every year for as long as he could remember, George and Jack celebrated each other's birthdays. But when Benny reached 75, he called Burns and told him he didn't want to go out. He wasn't feeling so great, he saw no reason to celebrate the fact that he was getting so old and closer to the end. He told Burns that he was just going to stay home, sip some wine, read a book and go to sleep early.

George had never heard his pal so melancholy and wanted to get him out of his funk. On the night of Benny's birthday, he was, indeed, sitting by himself, reading and sipping wine when the doorbell rang. Benny got up and opened the door, revealing his best buddy, George Burns. And standing behind Burns, in full uniform, was the entire UCLA marching band!

A whistle was blown and the band marched into Benny's house, drums banging and bugles blowing as they serenaded the astonished comedian with renditions of "Happy Birthday to You" and fight songs.

Benny burst out laughing and together the two friends happily celebrated Jack's birthday.

Someone asked George how much it cost to hire the marching band. George looked at the questioner like he was insane. "You can't put a price on friendship," he replied.

George was a member of Hillcrest Country Club, the same one Dad belonged to. They saw each other frequently as Dad played golf there several times a week and George played cards there every day. There is a plaque outside the card room at Hillcrest that reads: "No smoking allowed, unless you're over

90 years old!" It was put up especially for Burns and it still stands to this day.

Once, after Dad and I finished a round of golf, we were walking by the card room when Burns came out. He was carrying a martini in one hand and a cigar in the other. He and Dad greeted each other warmly and Dad asked him how old he was. Burns answered, "I'm 96." Dad said, "That's wonderful. But, George, I see that you're smoking and drinking. That can't be good for you. What does your doctor say about that?" Burns took a drag on his cigar, blew out the smoke and replied, "My doctor's dead!"

When my wife, Fran, was working at NBC as a game show writer, she was standing in front of an elevator at the studio when the doors opened and George Burns stepped out. Fran blurted out, "Oh, George Burns, I just love you!" George put his hands on both of her cheeks (the ones on her face) and replied, "I love you, too."

On Burns' 90th birthday, he was roasted at some swanky Beverly Hills Hotel. One of the roasters was my father and a couple of years ago, after Dad's passing, I found some notes scribbled on index cards that he used that night to roast George. Some of it is smudged and I believe a card or two is missing, but here are some of the remarks Dad made that hilarious evening:

"The year George Burns was born, the American flag only had thirteen stars."

"Movies and breakfast cereals were silent!"

"A basketball team consisted of five short white guys!"

"When he was still in his teens, George began smoking Coronas – not the cigar – the typewriter!"

"He was named after George Washington – but not long after!"

"The first time he voted for president, he registered as a Whig!"

"He once told Confucius to give up philosophy and go where the real money is – fortune cookies!"

"Little George was hooked on performing from the first time his parents took him to the theater. All right, it wasn't much of a show – a bunch of Christians being devoured by lions – but, hey, it was show business!"

"From 1922 to 1936, George teamed up with numerous partners as he tried to find the perfect combination that would please audiences. During those years he was one half of Burns and Shmolowitz, Burns and Tonto, Burns and Clarabelle, Burns and Trotsky, Burns and Rin-Tin-Tin – he tried everyone and everything – people, dogs, puppets, orthodox Rabbis..."

"Finally, he found her. She was funny and sexy and she was crazy about him. She had this adorable voice and she didn't even mind his cigars. George fell madly in love with her. He had it all figured out. They'd get married, travel all over America performing. They'd eventually have their own radio and TV shows. It would be a wonderful life. Unfortunately, Imogene Coca had other plans! So George settled for Gracie Allen!"

It was a wonderful night and George looked healthy and robust. My father expressed his desire to fete this American icon ten years hence.

Me with George Burns

Burns was supposed to perform at his 100th birthday show at Caesars Palace in Las Vegas, but he sustained a head injury from a bathroom fall and never fully recovered. Dad had bought tickets to see that show for the whole family, but the event was cancelled.

So George, wherever you are, on behalf of your legions of fans, my family and me, I just want to say, "We love you, too!"

SID CAESAR

Aside from my father, who I considered the funniest man alive, my concept of comedy was molded by the great comedian, Sid Caesar. As a kid, I would watch "Your Show of Shows," which Sid starred in, surrounded by a brilliant cast of zanies, including Carl Reiner, Imogene Coca and Howie Morris. It didn't hurt that his writing staff consisted of comedy legends like Mel Brooks, Neil Simon and Larry Gelbart.

One of my favorite sketches from that show opened with Sid sitting in a living room chair, holding a newspaper as far away as his arms could protrude, and squinting as he tried to read the print. Imogene Coca saw this and said: "Honey, why don't you get your eyes checked and get a pair of glasses?" His male ego challenged, Sid's character barked that his eyes were fine and that he didn't need glasses. He handed the paper to Coca and told her to walk to the end of the room and hold the paper up. He'd cover one eye and read the headline. Imogene walked to the other side of the room and held up the front page. In huge letters it proclaimed: "WORLD WAR TWO ENDS!" Sid grabbed a book of matches that was on the table and used it to cover an eye. He began to read, "C – L – O..." Coca shouted to him, "Where the heck do you see C – L – O?" Sid held up the book of matches and read, "Right here ... CLOSE COVER BEFORE STRIKING!"

Another time, Sid played Cool C, a hipster Jazz musician, wearing dark glasses and a small satellite dish on his head. Interviewed by Carl Reiner, he asked him what that was on his head. "It's radar. It warns me in case I get too close to a melody!"

And so it went, week after week, bringing new surprises that ingrained the lessons of comedy construction into my impressionable brain. So I felt extremely lucky that Dad invited Sid and his wife, Florence, to the house quite often. I got to see him at his manic best.

And he was manic, the poster child for ADD. The story about how he hung Mel Brooks out the window by his ankles on the fourteenth floor of the writer's room until he could come up with a joke that Sid liked, is true.

When Dad lived in a huge home in Rye, New York, he had a landscaper put in a whole new front lawn with flowers, trees and shrubs. He threw a dinner party for his friends, and when Sid showed up late, the driveway was already packed with cars. Not wanting to park far away, Caesar decided to get closer – by driving his car over the newly-sodded lawn, right up to the front door! Needless to say, he didn't get a lot of laughs that evening.

Much later in life, he was put on tranquilizing drugs that turned him into somewhat of a zombie. At one dinner party, I walked up to him and introduced myself. He smiled and extended his hand. "Hello, Warren, very nice to meet you." I was a bit startled since I'd known him since I was a little kid. We talked for over a half hour before we disengaged. An hour later, I saw him standing alone and approached him again. "Hi, Sid, are you enjoying the party?" "Yes," he responded, "very much so, uh, er ..." He looked at me blankly. "I'm Warren Murray, Sid." He gave me a big smile. "Hello, Warren, very nice to meet you."

Sid had a remarkable ability to talk in numerous dialects. What he said was gibberish – pure double-talk – but in foreign accents. It was brilliantly funny, and later in life, whenever he was asked to perform at a roast, he would get up and do his entire roast in accented double-talk.

One night, my father was being honored by the Friar's Club in Los Angeles, and they gave Dad a dinner/roast. (This is the same event that Milton Berle attended, as I alluded to earlier.) Don Rickles had just finished his roast remarks and the emcee announced: "And now, to say a few words about our guest of honor are the ambassadors from France, Italy, Japan and Russia!" The spotlight swung back to shine on the audience and Sid Caesar, as all four ambassadors, rose from his seat.

Sid was old then, and very frail. Two young caregivers flanked him, helping him to his feet and taking his arms to escort him to the stage. When the audience saw him initially, they burst into applause, but when they noticed how feeble he looked, a shocked gasp was emitted from everyone present. It seemed to take forever for him to reach the stage. When the two men stood him behind the podium, they retreated to either side of him in order to catch him if he started to fall. Sid was bent over, a pale shadow of the robust, muscular star we all remembered from "The Show of Shows."

The spotlight shined directly on him and an amazing transformation took place. He seemed to grow ten inches in height before our very eyes. In a powerful voice, he began to speak in gibberish-French, occasionally throwing in recognizable names like "Brigitte Bardot," "Eiffel Tower" and "Charles de Gaulle." Then he switched to other "ambassadors" and other dialects. By the time he finished, with a "Sayonara, Jan!" from the Japanese ambassador, the crowd was hysterical from laughing and gave Sid a standing ovation.

Dad, Me, Jack Carter and Sid Caesar

The spotlight swung away from him to the emcee and suddenly, Sid began to shrink back to the feeble old man who had walked to the stage. The two young men took him by the arms and practically carried him to his seat. It was a scene from "The Twilight Zone" and those who witnessed it were convinced that Sid was a robot who only came to life when the spotlight was on him.

Sayonara, Sid. You were one of the very best.

JACK CARTER

Jack Carter was a terrific comedian whose career spanned over 70 years. He was a star of TV, movies and nightclubs. And he was one of my Dad's closest friends. Jack had a deep, throaty voice that made him bark rather than talk. He also had a hair-trigger temper which exploded loudly, and with expletives that would make sailors blush.

This is probably why he was constantly turned down for golf memberships to country clubs all over Southern California. Whereas Dad and his golfing comedian friends all belonged to clubs, Jack was always turned down. Before being accepted for a golf membership, an applicant always had to play a round of golf with members of the membership committee. After 18 holes of cursing, throwing and breaking clubs, Jack was invariably voted down.

He could be a guest, though, and he played many times at Dad's invitation. On many occasions, I got to play with him, too. I must admit he kept me laughing whenever we played together, although I had to wash my ears out with soap after each round.

One time, a sexy bombshell actress from Brazil visited the United States and was asked who she'd like to have a romantic fling with in our country. She answered, "Paul Newman, Robert Redford, and Jack Carter." The interviewer was incredulous. "Why Jack Carter?" To which the actress replied, "Whenever anyone mentions him, they say, 'F__k Jack Carter!'"

Jack was always invited to our family Passover seder. For years he arrived with his second wife, actress Paula Stewart. Then they got divorced, and Jack called Dad and asked if he could bring a date to the upcoming seder. Dad told him it was fine, and on the night of the dinner, Jack showed up with a tall, blonde woman, wearing a tight-fitting dress that barely covered her enormous breasts. Jack introduced her to everyone and boasted, proudly, "She's the highest priced hooker in Los Angeles!"

Years later he married a beautiful, funny woman named Roxanne. One of her great traits was that she wouldn't take any crap from Jack. She did what everyone said was impossible – she domesticated him. Towards the end of his life, he seemed happier and mellower than he had ever been.

Still, the next time I hear a loud crack in the heavens, I'll have to ask myself, "Is that thunder? Or is it Jack Carter?"

CRUISING

My wife, Fran, and I have taken 40 cruises together. This, in itself, is somewhat of a miracle since Fran told me she'd never cruise because she got terribly seasick. This is a woman who takes Dramamine when she steps into a bathtub.

Modern cruise ships have state-of-the-art stabilizers so that you don't even know the ship is moving. But it wasn't always so. On a cruise with the now defunct Sitmar line, the ship I was on rode into a storm that made rock and roll more than a musical designation. The ship swayed so much I was afraid to yawn.

But I've ridden through storms in the newer ships, and I've never missed a meal. Cruise ships today are small cities, with up to 6,000 passengers and three or four pools. Some have rock climbing walls, water slide tubes and even zip lines. The showrooms produce Vegas-style extravaganzas and the casinos also take your money Vegas-style. The ships carry more food than the Marines had when they landed at Iwo Jima.

For years I gained a pound a day on every trip I took. When people asked me how long the cruise was that I booked, I'd answer, "It's a 12-pound cruise." And no wonder. With multiple dining rooms, 24-hour buffets, specialty restaurants, ice cream stands, room service and snack bars, passengers could eat from the moment they awakened until they went to bed. And if you were lucky enough to have a great room steward, he could even hook up an IV so they could pump food into you while you sleep!

Through the years, I've developed a system that prevents me from gaining weight on cruises. I only eat one meal a day. It starts at 7 A.M. and ends at midnight!

One of the first cruises I ever went on was 40-some years ago on the old Holland America ship, the Nieuw Amsterdam. All of their ships end in "Dam." There's the Rotterdam, the Veendam, the I Don't Give A Dam. I signed up for the passenger talent show as a standup comedian, and immediately panicked. What would I talk about? I had no act. Should I just steal jokes from my father? It was during my bout of anxiety that I began to notice "NO DUITGANG" signs posted all over the ship. I had no idea what they were warning passengers not to do, but it gave me an idea for my act. When I came out onstage I assumed an angry, snarling persona, a combination of Jack Carter and Don Rickles.

"I don't know about all of you," I barked at the audience, "but one of my favorite things to do in this whole world is to duitgang! You can imagine how upset I was when I saw 'NO DUITGANG' signs all over this ship! If I knew I wouldn't be allowed to duitgang, I wouldn't have booked this cruise in the first place! Since when can a cruise line tell two consenting adults that they can't duitgang? As soon as this show ends, my wife and I are going back to our stateroom and we're going to duitgang our brains out!"

I found out later that the sign meant "Emergency Exit." But, no one knew that. Everyone on board had seen the "NO DUITGANG" signs and wondered what they meant, too. The important thing was that they roared with laughter.

When I returned home, I told my dad about the experience. "Now I know how exhilarating it is to have wave after wave of laughter wash over you."

He rolled his eyes. "Oh, great, now I'll have to compete with YOU for club dates!"

One thing all cruises have in common is that they are always trying to sell you something – photographs, drinks, jewelry, refrigerator magnets – what a thrill it is to spend $10,000 to go to a floating swap meet!

For most of the cruises that Fran and I have taken, we've mostly gone on Princess. But when we wanted to go on the Fall Foliage Cruise along the East coast up to Canada, all the rooms we wanted on Princess were booked. My stepson, Steve, suggested we take Holland America. The new ships were clean, had great food and service, and most of all, they catered to seniors. Since Fran and I were both over 75 (even though we both think of ourselves as kids), the cruise sounded appealing. It would be nice to be on a cruise where loud teenagers didn't yell "MARCO! POLO!" for hours on end in the pool, or where we didn't have to listen to little kids run up and down the hallways screaming.

We booked the cruise and flew to Ft. Lauderdale. Upon entering the cruise terminal to check in, we knew immediately that Steve hadn't steered us wrong about the clientele of a Holland American cruise.

I had never seen so many wheelchairs, walkers, canes and oxygen tanks in my whole life. And that was just the crew!

I swear, the average age of the passengers was deceased!

Everyone kept calling me "Sonny."

Our stateroom was also tailored for seniors. The TV remote had two settings for volume – "Loud" and "Louder."

Instead of a hair dryer, our room came with a defibrillator!

At night, instead of placing chocolates on our pillows, our room steward left Metamucil!

The daily activities bulletin contained an obituary column!

We signed up for the late seating in the dining room. So there we were, at 3:30 – and seated next to a woman wearing a pin that proclaimed, "My great-great-great-great grandson is cuter than yours!"

She was there with her husband, who was attending a reunion of his old World War I buddies!

The first evening's big activity was an 80s Night – but we couldn't go – you had to actually be 80!

I have a hunch the captain himself was elderly. He steered the ship from Quebec to Montreal – with the left turn signal on the whole way!

Fran and me whale-watching in Cabo San Lucas

Okay, so I exaggerated a wee bit. I was a comedy writer and a Holland America cruise just screamed out for me to roast it. The truth is, we had a wonderful cruise and if post-pandemic cruising is truly safe enough to do again, Fran and I will continue going on them, from sea to shining sea.

DAD (JAN MURRAY)

Dad was born Murray Leon Janofsky. His parents, my paternal grandparents, were born in a small town on the border between Poland and Russia. They were either Polish or Russian, depending on who was winning the war that week.

When they arrived at Ellis Island and the clerk asked for their name, they uttered something that was totally incomprehensible, so the clerk wrote down "Janofsky." My grandmother was appalled. Janofsky wasn't even close to their real name. Offended, she insisted that everyone call her "Mrs. J." The immigrant couple had two children in America. One was my uncle, David. He shortened his last name to "Janoff" which sounded more American to him without the "sky." And my father was Murray Janofsky, until he decided to go into show business and his agent told him to Americanize his name. "You can't have Murray Janofsky on a marquee," the agent told him. "People will think they're coming to see a Polish western!" So Dad shortened Janofsky to "Jan", and made it his first name, while moving "Murray" to the rear, as his new last name. He was now Jan Murray. From that time on, whenever the whole family got together they'd be introduced, "This is Mr. Janofsky, his wife, Mrs. J. and their two children, Dave Janoff and Jan Murray!"

Later in life, Dad mentioned on his TV show, "Treasure Hunt," that he had gone to school at DeWitt Clinton High School in the Bronx. A week later, the principal of that school called him to ask why he'd lie about attending Clinton. He had checked all the files and no one named Jan Murray had ever graduated from there. Dad explained that when he attended, his name was Murray Janofsky and he never graduated because he had to go to work to help support the family during the depression. The principal said he'd like to offer Dad an honorary high school diploma – if he'd speak at that year's graduation. Dad agreed. The day before his big event was my college graduation from NYU. So on Friday, Dad attended my college graduation and on Saturday, I went to his high school graduation!

My parents divorced when I was a small child. I lived with my mother, Pearl, in Brooklyn, while Dad bought his first house in Woodmere, Long Island, with his new wife, Toni. I saw him on weekends and holidays. For several years he would drive into Brooklyn and pick me up. (Later, he had his chauffeur pick me up.) It was during one of the times when Dad drove in that he told me the first joke I can ever remember hearing.

We were driving to Long Island and it started to rain heavily. I commented that it was "raining cats and dogs." Dad responded, "I know. I stepped in a poodle!" To a six-year-old, this was the funniest thing I had ever heard. I began laughing uncontrollably, all the way to Long Island. In school on Monday, I must have repeated that joke a zillion times, getting big laughs from my classmates. I didn't know it at the time, but I was experiencing first-hand the addictive power of humor.

I never understood what Dad did for a living when I was a kid. A plumber was a job. A teacher was a job. "Making people laugh" just didn't seem like a real job to me.

Dad was booked into Ben Maksik's Town and Country Club, the largest night club in Brooklyn. He had never played it before and wanted to get the lay of the land of the venue he was going to perform in for a whole week. He took me with him backstage, where we watched the young pop singer Bobby Vinton finish his set on his closing night. When he concluded his final song, "Mr. Blue," dozens of teenage girls shrieked, screamed and tried to rush the stage. Vinton blew them kisses and waved to his adoring fans. Most of the crowd filed out, but a sizable contingent of teenage girls stayed behind. Dad and I figured they were hoping Vinton would come back out and give them autographs. After a while, the singer did emerge. He went over to the girls, thanked them for a job well done – and gave each of them a ten-dollar bill!

The next night, Dad opened at the club to a full house. I sat up front with the family. It was the first time I ever saw Dad perform onstage. For over an hour he belted out jokes to thunderous laughter. When it was over, he was given a standing ovation. Backstage, Dad asked me how I felt about what I had just seen. I replied, "Now I know what you do for a living!" Dad laughed and I continued. "Just one question – did you have to pay all those people ten dollars?" Dad shrieked with laughter and retold that story to his friends for many years.

Dad and me at age four

Dad, like most comedians of his day, did a lot of jokes about his wife and kids. Since my two sisters and brother hadn't been born yet, he focused all of his "kid jokes" on me. Most of the lines have long faded from my memory, but I remember a few:

"My son, Warren, is so wild and obnoxious, I hired another kid to play him in my home movies!"

"I once told Warren he could be anything he wants to be. My luck, he wants to be an idiot!"

"I'm not kidding. Last week he asked his mother, 'Are you the opposite sex, or am I?'"

My father didn't suffer fools real well, even if they were family members. Whenever I did something he didn't approve of, he would always shake his finger at me and ask, "What are you, an idiot?" After a lifetime of hearing that accusatory question, I finally blew up at him. "Dad," I growled. "I'm married. I have kids. I support myself. I'm 40 years old. I really resent you calling me an idiot!" Dad thought about it for perhaps a full second, before he proclaimed, lovingly, "When you're 70, I'll be 94. I'll still be your father and you'll still be an idiot!"

When Dad became wealthy, he bought a 14-room estate in Rye, New York, on the grounds of the Westchester Country Club. His next door neighbor was John Daly, the host of the popular "What's My Line?" TV show. Dad was an avid golfer and would love to have joined the Westchester club, but it was restricted. No Jews were allowed to be members. Dad could only play golf there if a member invited him. Luckily, he was good friends with a member, Ed Sullivan, and Ed invited him to play quite often.

Dad always joked, "I can play golf there. I just can't shower there!"

Dad gave me lots of gifts through the years, but the strangest one occurred on my 18th birthday. To understand the nature and intent of this gift, let me give you some background. When my father changed his name from Murray Janofsky to Jan Murray, a very gentile-sounding name, he decided to change his appearance, too, to fit his new name. So he had a friend of his, Sam Scheer, a renowned plastic surgeon make him a new nose.

Murray Janofsky nose and Jan Murray nose

My graduation gift from him was, you guessed it, a new nose! I never asked for it. I never even considered it. But Dad wanted me to look like a Murray, not a Janofsky, so like it or not, I was getting a new nose.

High school nose and College nose

I must admit that with my new nose, my self-confidence grew and since no one at NYU (and later, Columbia) ever knew me with my old schnoz, I became much more popular with the opposite sex. It was a gift that has lasted a lifetime and one that I didn't have to return or re-gift.

On Dad's 80th birthday, a big party was thrown for him at The Improv in Hollywood. All of Dad's family and friends attended. There was Buddy Hackett, Milton Berle, Jerry Lewis, Shecky Green, Sid Caesar and dozens of other comics, actors and singers that had filled his home and his life. Each got up and "roasted" him, lovingly. During the show, Dad turned to me and said he'd like me to get up and say a few words.

Talk about panic. I had to stand in front of the pantheon of American comedy and try to be funny. I ran to the men's room and quickly started to jot down notes as fast as I could. Somewhere in the night I was introduced. I don't remember everything I said that night, but some remarks still come to me:

"I'm really proud of you, Dad. Your career has spanned over 60 years and every genre of show business. You've starred in television, radio, movies, nightclubs, burlesque, vaudeville, minstrel shows, covered wagons, Roman orgies and public hangings!"

"And even though Bob Hope gets most of the credit for entertaining American troops, I want all of you who are present tonight to know that during World War II, Dad entertained more than 300,000 troops." (The crowd erupted into thunderous applause.) "Unfortunately," I continued, "they were German Prisoners of War!"

"Oh, before I forget, someone slipped me a note to read to you before I went on." (I took out a crumpled note from my pocket, opened it and read): "From the Los Angeles Primate Preserve – Congratulations, Jan, you're a father again!"

"It's really something to have a father who has his own star on the Hollywood Walk of Fame. Imagine, my own father immortalized in cement – right next to Jimmy Hoffa!"

"I've gotten so much from you, Dad – headaches,

ulcers and a prostate that's so large, I haven't peed since January!"

"When I was a teenager, I got really tired of being called 'Jan Murray's son." When I met a girl, I'd say, "Hi. I'm Warren Murray and I'm in your English class. Would you like to go out on a date with me?" If she said "No," I'd quickly add: "Did I mention I'm Jan Murray's son?!" Amazingly, more often than not, the girl would change her mind and go out with me. So thank you, Dad. You may not know this about yourself but – you're a chick magnet!"

Me performing at Dad's 80th

"In closing, let me state emphatically, Dad, that I've gotten all of my values from you. I'll never forget you telling me that all of us were put on this earth to help others. So, I only have one question for you – what were the OTHERS put here for?"

"Happy Birthday, Dad, I love you."

Dad passed away in 2006 at the age of 89. In keeping with his wishes, he asked everyone to "roast" him at his funeral. Even in death, he found THE FUNNY SIDE.

DIETING

I've been dieting seemingly my whole life. At home, I have three wardrobes for when I'm fat, skinny and in the middle – either on the way up or down. If you counted all the pounds I've gained and lost through the years on my myriad of diets, it's over 100,000 pounds. I stay on a diet about as long as Venus De Milo can stay on a pogo stick!

To tell the truth, my stomach was always flat – it's just that the "L" was silent!

I've tried every diet that's ever come out. I've been on Jenny Craig more than Mister Craig!

I took the Oprah Winfrey two-week diet and lost 14 days!

I went on the banana and coconut diet. I didn't lose any weight, but, boy, could I climb a tree!

One of my diets said I should liquefy everything before eating. One night I drank three lamb chops and a corn-on-the-cob!

As part of a diet, I took up exercising by riding horses. It worked. In three weeks the horse lost 18 pounds!

Many diet programs require you to stay on them for many years. I tried Weight Watchers, but the only thing I lost was my patience!

One diet I went on consisted of eating vegetables and drinking wine. Within two weeks I lost six pounds and my driver's license!

A friend of mine tried a diet that only allowed him to use sugar substitutes. Two years later he died from artificial diabetes!

I never eat between meals because for me, there is no between meals!

I've learned that you can lose weight by simply giving up two things – a knife and a fork!

I don't mean to brag, but I once finished a 14-day diet in two hours and 12 minutes!

Here's the best diet – only eat when the news is good!

Have you noticed they never advertise celery on TV?

I have a theory that you can lose weight through acupuncture. Whenever you eat food – it leaks out!

What a country. We spend half our money on food – and the other half on diets.

I tried a diet where all I ate was fish. After a month, I started to breathe through my cheeks!

My wife started a new diet but quickly switched to another one. The first one didn't give her enough to eat!

That reminds me, a recent study found that wives who carry a little extra weight live longer than the husbands who mention it!

Helpful diet hint – eat all you want – chew – but don't swallow!

Another hint – move your scale from the bathroom to in front of the refrigerator!

I gave up on the onion diet. I lost eight pounds – and 12 friends!

My 300-pound friend claims there's nothing wrong with his weight, it's his HEIGHT that's wrong. He should be 8' 2"!

I have another friend who eats everything and never gains an ounce. A typical meal for him consists of two steaks, a baked potato with sour cream, three scoops of ice cream, a slice of chocolate cake and a malted. Incredibly, he still weighs the same 462 pounds!

I know dieting isn't easy. Let's face it – the waist is a terrible thing to mind!

Enough. The comedy writer in me forces me to automatically find the funny side of any topic I'm talking about. The truth is, dieting isn't so funny when we're dieting. We have to give up a lot of food that clogs our arteries and strains our heart muscles. The upside is that we will feel healthier and live longer. This is a good trade off to me. Since the pandemic started more than a year ago, I've been on a diet and exercise program that has resulted in me having more energy and a better torso than I've had in 50 years. Before I started this regimen, I was so heavy that every time I backed up, I beeped! In the past year I've lost 35 pounds and have kept it off. How do I look now that I've shed all that weight? My wife recently told me, "You're not half the man you used to be!"

How did I do it? I walk three miles a day and I've cut way down on my carbs and calories. I write down everything I eat and plan my whole day's diet the night before. Once I reach my allotted calories and carbs, I resolutely refuse to go over those figures. What is my goal? I was told to keep it realistic, so, ultimately, I want to be able to walk through a harp!

I realize I may sound like a hypochondriac to you. Even several of my doctors have accused me of being a hypochondriac – including my gynecologist!

But it all boils down to me wanting to live longer and healthier. Dieting is a big part of that. But you have to WANT to lose weight. The secret to losing weight, at least for me, is to eat LESS. As long as I stay within my goals for the day, I can eat anything I want, even BAD foods, like ice cream, bagels and pasta. I just don't eat MOUNTAINS of them like I use to. Do I resent cutting way back or sometimes completely on the foods I used to devour? To answer that, let me quote a story my dad used to tell in his act.

An elderly man goes to the doctor and whines, "I can't pee."

The doctor asks, "How old are you?"

The old man answers, "I'm 92."

The doctor tells him, "You've peed enough!"

And so, dear reader, when it comes to junk food, the truth is that at 79, I've eaten enough!

I sincerely hope that I can sustain my new regimen, especially after restaurants open again. If I can't, I vow to keep trying new diet programs and stick with them – through thick and thin!

GOLF

I've been playing golf since I was 14. However, unlike wine, golfers don't improve with age. If I swung my clubs now the way I did 65 years ago, I'd be in traction for a month. My swing speed is so slow, Stephen Hawking could've out-driven me.

In my garage I have 16 putters and three full sets of clubs. When my game goes south, I never blame it on my swing. It must be the equipment. I'm always positive that the next club I purchase will miraculously fix my game.

At 79, I've settled into an old man's game. I've lost a great deal of distance, but I've learned how to hit the ball straight. I'm always in play and if I can chip and putt well, I can still get a good score. My new game has an added benefit. It saves me lots of money on golf balls. I simply don't hit them far enough to lose them!

I've played all over the United States and more than a dozen courses in Southern California. My "home" course is Westlake Village Golf Club. I always walk the entire 18 holes, pushing my four-wheeled golf cart in front of me. I'm frequently paired with young men who outdrive me by a football field, but for their second shots, they often have to use a machete! Instead of caddies, they need Sherpa guides! They can never understand how the old guy reaches the green before them. It's simple – I play "closest to the course."

Still, I envy those apes who can smack the ball 300 yards. If I could do that, even once, I'd throw a block party! I played with a 20-something one day and watched him drive the green on a par-4 hole! I said to him, "Didn't I see you on top of the Empire State Building, swatting airplanes?" He was so young, he had no idea I was referencing King Kong. This happens to me a lot these days. Once, on the 7th tee at Westlake, I mentioned to a young man that I had met the great Aussie tennis legend Rod Laver right on that spot 25 years earlier. His eyes glazed over. "Who's Rod Laver?" he asked. As I extracted the knife from my heart, I explained it to him. He was unimpressed. "Oh. Whatever."

And these young guys always ride in electric carts while the old fart walks. The only older man I ever saw riding a cart was named Fred. He was 94 and hit every ball 100 yards. He was always in play and could still chip and putt. On the 14th tee, I hit a high drive, looked up to watch it, and lost the ball in the sun. I told Fred I didn't even see what direction it went so I was going to hit another ball. Fred said, "No need to hit another one. I saw it."

I was incredulous. "You saw it?!"

He answered, "Sure. Why are you so surprised?"

I reminded him that he was 94 and that people his age often had eye problems. He just laughed. "I just had cataract surgery," he proclaimed, "and they gave me new lenses. I have 20-20 vision for the first time in over six decades."

"That's great," I responded, impressed. "So, where's my ball?"

He looked down the fairway and announced, "I don't remember!"

I laughed for the rest of the round. Fred was quite funny and was a bit of a philosopher, too. When the round ended, I asked him what his score was. It's very unusual for a man of his age to break (shoot lower than) 100 and I was curious to know if he had done it. Fred looked over his scorecard and proudly proclaimed, "I got a 32!"

"A 32?" I shouted. "What kind of a score is 32?"

He put his hand on my shoulder and answered with a twinkle, "At my age, I only count the GOOD ones!"

That's not a bad philosophy for all us duffers. Trying to shoot a low score can be humbling for septuagenarians like me. Many's the time I've finished a round and one of my playing partners has asked me what I shot. More often than I'd like, I've answered, "I hope to live to that age! "These days, my goal is to "shoot my age" (79). Mostly, though, I end up shooting my weight!

When I was 56 years old, I shot a 68. I didn't break 70 again until I was 76. That year, my score was 69. I usually shoot in the high 70s to low 80s, which isn't bad for an old coot.

I've never had a hole-in-one, although I've come very close several times. Two weeks ago, on a par 3, I just missed a hole-in-one – by two...shots!

I was recently accepted for membership in the PGA. (The Pathetic Golfer's Association!)

My wife still can't understand how a grown man can waste four hours of his life chasing after a little white ball. The answer is simple. Golf is a challenge. I get to meet many interesting people. Since no two courses are the same, the surroundings are often breathtaking. It's cheaper than therapy. (You go from euphoria to depression and back a dozen times a round.) And finally, golf is the only game where a man can spend endless hours with "hookers," and not have his wife complain!

That's not entirely true. I recall Fran snapping at me, "You're so involved with golf, you don't even remember the day we were married!" To which I replied, "Sure I do. It was the day I sank a fifty-foot putt!"

I've played golf with numerous celebrities, including Milton Berle, Jack Carter, Buddy Hackett, Hal March, Joey Bishop, Donnie Most, Rob Riggle, Eddie Money, Gary Sinese, Harvey Korman and Frankie Avalon, to name a few.

I even played a round of golf with O.J. Simpson at Monarch Beach, a few years before his notorious murder trial. Surrounded by stars my whole life, I was never overly impressed or intimidated by playing golf with celebrities. The one exception came when I went out to play as a "single" and was told to pair up with the gentleman on the first tee. Upon reaching him, I saw a tall, muscular black gentleman and shook hands with him. His hand was the size of a tree stump. I commented that he had the hands of an athlete. He replied that he had been a major league pitcher. "I'm Don Newcombe."

Me with Frankie Avalon at a Riviera Country Club celebrity golf charity fundraiser

Growing up in Brooklyn and watching him and the other "Boys of Summer" (Jackie Robinson, Duke Snider, Roy Campanella, Gil Hodges, Pee Wee Reese and Carl Furillo), Newk was one of my idols. Instead of saying, "Glad to meet you. I'm Warren Murray." I blurted out, "Hamana hamana hamana, hamana!" He must have thought he was playing with an orangutan.

My father was right when he bought me golf lessons for my 14th birthday and told me it was something I could do for the rest of my life. Every round brings new challenges and, more importantly, new stories to tell. I intend to keep on playing as long as I'm still on this side of the grass.

I say this knowing full well that golf is the most exasperating game ever invented. The only reason it's called "golf," is that all the other four-letter words were taken!

Still, despite all the balls I've lost in lakes and woods, all the greens I've three-putted and all the money I've spent on green fees, carts, equipment and lessons, all of these negatives are cancelled out by one immutable truth: Golf is the most fun you can have without taking your clothes off!

Me at the famous third hole at Mauna Kea on the Big Island

BUDDY HACKETT

Buddy Hackett (born Leonard Hacker) was my dad's closest friend and arguably one of the funniest comedians who ever lived. My father always lamented the fact that at 6' 2", muscular, with a full head of dark, wavy hair, he always had to go onstage in front of an audience looking more like a movie star than a comedian. He had to work hard to get the folks to laugh. Buddy, on the other hand, was short, round and talked with almost a childlike voice. The minute he came onstage, even before he said a word, the audience was laughing.

You might remember Buddy from his very early TV show "Stanley," or from when he sang "Shipoopi" in the movie version of "The Music Man." To this day, you can go on YouTube and watch his many classic appearances with Johnny Carson on the "Tonight Show." But his true brilliance was on display for the many decades he headlined in Las Vegas.

His audience was always packed. As was the custom in the 50s and 60s, performers did two shows a night: the dinner show and the late show. One night, at the dinner show, Buddy told his audience, "Hey, everybody. My good friend Jan Murray is playing at the Riviera tonight. He's really funny. You wanna do something really great? Tonight, after my show, why don't you all go over to see Jan. And no matter how funny he is – no matter how much you want to – DON'T LAUGH!"

That night, at the 10 o'clock show, Dad went on and told his first joke. He had gotten huge laughs with it at the dinner show and was stunned when the whole audience stared back at him in total silence.

He banged the microphone. "Hello? Hello? Is this thing on?" Then he told his second joke, also to silence. "Do any of you speak English?!" he shouted to the audience. Again, nothing. He told his third joke and once more you could hear a pin drop. "What are you, an oil painting?!" By now sweat was pouring down his face.

From somewhere in the darkness boomed the unmistakable voice of Buddy Hackett. "Hi, Jan! How's it going so far?!"

"SONOFABITCH!" Dad bellowed. "You sent them here and told them not to laugh, didn't you?!"

The entire audience erupted into a thunderous explosion of laughter.

Buddy joined Dad onstage and together the two of them did an unrehearsed, impromptu performance for well over an hour that Vegas oldtimers still talk about to this day.

As a teenager, I joined Buddy and Dad on the golf course many times, but the most memorable round I recall happened at a course in Ft. Lee, New Jersey when I was 15. The three of us teed off together, and on the 8th hole, Buddy sliced his drive deep into the woods. This wasn't just a few scraggly trees, it was the Amazon rainforest. There was no way we were going to find his ball.

"Put another ball down, Buddy," Dad prompted, "that one's gone."

"I paid a buck for that ball and I'm gonna find it," Buddy announced. He started walking towards the woods.

"Are you crazy?" Dad called out. "The ball's lost. You're going to hold up the entire course. Look, here's a dollar. You can buy yourself a new ball after we're done."

But Buddy, seemingly not listening, disappeared into the woods. Dad and I kept calling out to him, but got no answer. We eventually had to let two foursomes play through us. Dad got angrier and more frustrated. Finally, he exploded.

"Buddy!" he screamed, "If you don't come out right now, Warren and I are playing on without you!"

A second passed and Buddy re-emerged from the woods – stark naked! He didn't have one ounce of clothing on him! And as Dad and I stared at him in shocked disbelief, Buddy "explained" what happened to him with one word:

"LOCUSTS!!!!!"

Buddy passed away shortly before my father. While my dad was fading fast, I asked him if he believed in the afterlife. He said he did and he was looking forward to seeing his brother and his parents again. But most of all, he hoped that he'd be able to play some heavenly golf and share some laughter once more with Buddy. Given how badly Hackett played, the next time I hear a booming voice from high above shout, "FORE!," I'll know it's just Buddy, still searching for his ball.

Buddy Hackett, in the woods at Vernon Hills Country Club, Mt. Vernon, N.Y. in 1958

"HOLLYWOOD SQUARES"

The original version of "Hollywood Squares" ran on NBC from 1966 to 1980. Based on Tic-Tac-Toe, nine celebrities were seated inside a gigantic tower and answered questions put to them by the show's host, Peter Marshall. Two contestants tried to get Tic-Tac-Toe, and the way they got it was to take turns calling on a star and then either agreed or disagreed with that star's answer. The show's creators, Merrill Heatter and Bob Quigley, added a FUNNY SIDE to the game by having each star ad-lib a joke answer before actually giving a real answer to the question posed to them. People tuned in more for the jokes than for the game itself. It became so popular, they added a primetime version that ran while the show cranked out episodes daily for 14 years.

The present-day show, "Funny You Should Ask," uses the same exact formula except for the tic-tac-toe game. However, the show that started this genre was the original "Hollywood Squares," and I was lucky enough to be a small part of its history.

The regulars on "Squares," who appeared on every episode, were Wally Cox, the mild-mannered comic actor who was the voice of the children's cartoon "Underdog" and also starred in his own early TV sitcom, "Mr. Peepers." Seated next to him was the wonderful comic actress Rose Marie. Best remembered from her recurring role on "The Dick Van Dyke Show," she was a veteran of motion pictures. In the bottom left square was the hilarious

Cliff Arquette, who always appeared on the show, in character, as Charley Weaver from Mt. Idy. If there was a breakout star on "Squares," it was Paul Lynde. Paul was a star of movies and Broadway. He always sounded like he was being put upon and he had a way of delivering one-liners in a whiny voice that was uniquely his own.

My father was a semi-regular, appearing on roughly half of the episodes each year. The other four spots were usually reserved for guest celebrities. It became a big deal to appear on "Hollywood Squares," similar to being chosen to perform on "The Tonight Show." If you were on "Squares," it meant you had made it, you were somebody.

In 1969, I was living in California and working as an insurance underwriter as part of their Management Trainee Program. Before that, I had been a tenured teacher in Spring Valley, New York, and also taught at Crescenta Valley High in La Crescenta, California. I had moved to California to become a comedy writer, but after a year and a half, nothing had happened. I was married to my first wife and had an infant son to support. I was living in a small apartment, making $8,000 a year and wondering if I had made a mistake upending everyone's lives to follow my California dream.

And then I caught a break. One of the writers on "Hollywood Squares" quit the show and my father, who was close friends with the producers, recommended me to take the place of the guy who left. Since I had no experience, the producers agreed to give me a ten-week tryout at $300 a week. If I worked out, I'd be given a one-year contract at double that. I jumped at the chance to earn five times what I was making at Allstate, but it was a gamble. If I left the Management Trainee Program at the insurance giant, I'd never be asked back. And if I flopped as a game show writer, I'd be out of work with a family to support.

I took the job.

Being a former teacher, I assumed I'd be researching the questions to be asked the stars. Imagine my shock when I was told my job would be to write the AD-LIBS for the stars! It was explained to me that I'd be given that night's questions to be asked to one or more celebrities, and I was tasked with writing the joke that the star would blurt out, seemingly off the top of their head.

I asked who I was writing for on the next night's show, and I was told it was Paul Lynde! I couldn't believe it. I had never done anything like this before and they were throwing me into the deep end of the pool. The producer confided to me that the other writers wanted no part of Paul, who often hated his "ad-libs" and wasn't afraid to share his displeasure with the frightened writer who "dared passing off this crap as a joke."

Suddenly, my job, my career and possibly my marriage depended on Paul's reaction to what I wrote.

That night I pored over the questions that Paul would be asked at the next taping and bravely tried to come up with joke ad-libs, constantly second-guessing myself to the point where I never went to sleep the entire night. When I handed in my ad-libs, the producer glanced over them, smiled and even chuckled a few times and told me, "I like them, but it all comes down to whether Paul likes them."

The ad-libs for all the celebrities were taped to the desktops of their boxes and I waited backstage for the stars to take their places. Each was introduced to the studio audience. Some waved. Some told a joke. Lynde was a waver.

He sat down and glanced at the material I had written. Instantly, his eyes grew large and the blood disappeared from his face. He called over the producer. I moved closer in the wings so I could hear their conversation.

Paul said, "My first ad-lib is only one word."

The producer nodded. "Correct. But it's funny."

Paul persisted. "It's only one word. If it doesn't get a laugh, I'll be hung out to dry."

The producer assured him it was funny, but Paul wasn't convinced. "Who wrote this?" Paul demanded.

"The kid."

(Note – at one time in my life I was "The Kid.")

Paul hissed, "Send him over to me."

Before I could hide, the producer spotted me and motioned that I should come over to him. "Mr. Lynde wants to ask you something," he said, just before he scampered off backstage and out of harm's way.

"You wanted to see me, Mr. Lynde?" I asked with trepidation.

"The first joke only has one word!" he scolded.

I'll never understand why I did what I did next, but I looked Paul Lynde right in the eye and proclaimed, "If you don't get a huge laugh with that word, you can fire me on the spot!"

Paul shot me an evil smile and warned, "I'm going to hold you to that, kid."

I gulped and went back to the wings in a daze. What I thought was bravado on my part had actually been stupidity. If Lynde didn't get a big laugh, I'd be out of work. People would ask me years later how long I worked in show business and my reply would be, "One word."

The show began and just to add to my misery, Lynde was the last to be called. Peter Marshall asked, "For the win, Paul, why would a man pound his meat?"

The real answer, of course, was to tenderize it. But I didn't care about the real answer, only my joke. The question itself was suggestive and got a laugh from the audience and the other celebrities. Marshall continued, after the laugh, mostly to set up the joke again. "Once again, Paul, why would a man pound his meat?

Paul stared right into the camera and answered, "LONELINESS!"

The entire studio exploded into thunderous laughter. The cameramen laughed so hard, the cameras shook. The stars in the other boxes shrieked and pounded the tops of their desks. And in the midst of all this pandemonium, Paul Lynde sneaked a peek at me backstage and gave me a "thumbs up."

I was officially in show business.

As a footnote to this story, several months later, Marlo Thomas, the daughter of one of Dad's closest friends, Danny Thomas, appeared on the show. Marlo was starring in a new sitcom called "That Girl." I was assigned to write the ad-libs for her and evidently she was pleased with the laughs she received. She asked the producer to send over the writer and I appeared.

She asked if I had ever written a full 42-page half-hour TV sitcom script before and I shook my head "no." She explained that she was starting a new show and was looking for some talented young writers. Would I mind, she inquired, if she sent me few finished scripts to look at? "After you read them," she added, "if you think this is something you can do, call my producers and they'll set up an appointment for you to pitch story ideas to them. If they like one, they'll give you an assignment."

Well, I read the scripts, came up with some episodic plot lines, called the producers, and sold them the first one I pitched. They loved the script and I wound up writing multiple episodes of "That Girl." From that time on, for more than the next two decades, I wrote scripts for over 40 shows, including such hits as "All In the Family," "Happy Days," "Alice," "The Facts of Life," "Diff'rent Strokes," "Bridget Loves Bernie," "Room 222," "Love, American Style" and so many others. It was an exciting, lucrative and creative career, and I owe it all to:

"LONELINESS!"

INVENTIONS

There is no doubt that Man has been inventing things since we began to stand upright. There have been big inventions that changed the world completely, like the telephone, electricity, the computer, cars, trains, planes and rocket ships.

All of those altered the way we communicated, traveled and interacted with each other. But don't sell short other inventions that have made our lives less complicated and more sanitary, like the flip-top can and toilet paper. We revere inventors like Thomas Edison, Alexander Graham Bell and Ben Franklin, but where are the accolades for Sir Thomas Crapper, who invented the flush toilet? Saying "I'm going to the crapper," or "I have to take a crap," doesn't seem to be a fitting tribute to a man whose invention benefits all mankind.

There's a chain of stores called "As Seen on TV" that sells items that garage inventors were sure would revolutionize the world and, coincidently, make them millions of dollars. The TV ads or infomercials hawking these products can be seen at 3 A.M. on off-channels everywhere. Most are "improvements" on existing inventions. They talk in glowing terms of a better mouse trap, a better mop, a better frying pan, etc. It's possible they are better, but very few of them have modified how people cook, clean, disinfect, or smell to the extent their inventors hoped for.

Someone once said that "necessity is the mother

of invention." When we needed a better way to see, someone made a light bulb. But some inventors have made fortunes inventing things that fill no discernible void. Do we really need a Hula Hoop? A Pet Rock? A Lava Lamp? A Mood Ring? A Frisbee? A Chia Pet? A Slinky? These silly diversions made millions for their creators as the masses stormed their neighborhood stores to make sure they got theirs before they sold out.

I've often wondered if I've wasted my time writing and teaching when I could have become filthy rich as an inventor. Think about it. As a writer I create characters, plots and jokes. Why couldn't I use that creativity to come up with a multi-million-dollar invention?

So for the last month, I've spent my time trying to think of the next sure-fire invention that will put me on Easy Street for the remainder of my life. Here is a partial list of some of my can't-miss inventions:

A book on How to Read!

Re-useable ice cubes!

A dictionary index!

Pedal-powered wheelchairs!

Skinless bananas!

A revolving basement restaurant!

Powdered water!

A waterproof tea bag!

An inflatable dart board!

Chocolate-covered lox on a stick!

A glass-bottomed airplane for flying over nudist camps!

A Valium Suppository for "peace" of ass!

Okay, I stole the last one from Redd Foxx. But the point of this futile exercise is that comedy writers make lousy inventors. Given a choice of doing something to improve the human condition or make someone laugh, we'll always go for the laugh.

I have a lot more to say on this subject, but it'll have to wait for my next book because right now – I have to go to the crapper!

LAS VEGAS

The Las Vegas I remember from my youth doesn't exist anymore. Wonderful hotels like the Sands, the Dunes, the Hacienda, the Sahara, the Riviera, the Desert Inn, the Thunderbird, the Frontier and more than a dozen other hotel/casinos have long since been blown to smithereens to make room for taller, more modern structures.

My first wife and I once drove to the Strip in Las Vegas. Dolly Parton was performing at the Riviera Hotel and we hoped to catch her dinner show. Unfortunately, there were some conventions in town and the only room we could find was in the dilapidated El Rancho.

Somehow I was able to get us in to see Dolly and she was terrific. Noted for her curvy figure as well as for being a country music superstar, she came out on stage and immediately addressed the crowd, "Well, Howdy, everyone! My, look at all the men in the front row! I've never seen so many binoculars!" After the audience stopped laughing, she added, "Listen everyone, they're mine and they're real! Now that I've addressed what's on all your minds, who'd like to hear some really great music?" The audience cheered, there were no more boob jokes, and the music really was great.

Back at our hotel, we gambled a bit and went to bed. At 2 A.M. the emergency horn sounded loudly in our room, and lights flashed on and off. I opened the door and saw people scurrying quickly down the hallway in their night clothes. We threw on our robes and rushed down the staircase to the street, exiting through a rear door. There were now hundreds of people from the hotel standing on Las Vegas Boulevard in various stages of undress. We all waited around for the fire trucks and ambulances, but after fifteen minutes, none arrived. I finally walked into the hotel and found the lights on, people gambling and no one rushing for the exits. I found a hotel clerk at the check-in window and asked him if the all-clear had sounded. He stared at me, puzzled. "What all-clear? And why are you in your pajamas and a robe?" I explained that the room alarms had sounded and there were hundreds of guests in the street. He seemed more annoyed than shocked. "That damn electrical system shorted out again!" he thundered. "Tell everyone to go back to their rooms. There's no fire."

I relayed his message to the throng. The message was greeted with a combination of relief and cursing. My wife and I returned to our room, fell asleep and an hour later – the alarms went off again! We were now in a "Boy Who Cried Wolf" quandary. Was this another case of crossed wires, or the real thing? Luckily, the room phone still worked. I called down immediately and was told it was another false alarm.

In the morning, I tried to get my money back for the scare and the inconvenience. The manager said he wasn't authorized to do that. I became irate and told him I was never staying at the El Rancho ever again, and that I was contacting my lawyer when I got home. He just shrugged and turned away.

Two weeks later, the El Rancho was imploded with high explosives.

I took my second wife to Las Vegas and we stayed at Caesars Palace. In those days, Caesars held their breakfast/lunch buffet in the main showroom, onstage. When we arrived to eat there was a huge line and an almost one-hour wait. While I stood in line, she seated herself in front of a quarter machine. After a few pulls, I heard the unmistakable Ding-Ding-Ding, denoting a jackpot! Coins tumbled into the slot and she gathered them up and tossed them into a plastic container. A few minutes later, she hit another jackpot, then another. By the time I made it to fourth in line, I signaled her to stop playing and join me, so we could eat. Understandably, she didn't want to leave her cash cow, but, reluctantly, she got up, holding two enormous cups filled with quarters. Before she could take ten steps towards me, several casino employees descended on her machine and unscrewed it from its moors. Overseen by two "Men in Black," the machine was lifted up and carried away, presumably to be taken for a ride, beaten to pieces with a baseball bat, and buried in the desert.

The truth is, the House almost always comes out ahead in the casinos. They couldn't stay in business if they lost regularly. I've been approached by losers every time I've been to Vegas. The old joke is that a guy arrives in Vegas driving a $30,000 car – and goes home in a $600,000 bus! The last time I was on the

Strip, a panhandler approached me and asked me for $5 so he could buy some food. I asked, suspiciously, "How do I know you won't spend the five bucks on gambling?" He answered, "Hey, I've GOT gambling money!"

Vegas has tried to reinvent itself through the years. At first, the Mob made it a Mecca for high rollers to indulge in gambling, shows, food and ladies of the night. This persisted until someone decided to make it more family-friendly. Amusement parks were built, along with arcades, day-care centers and babysitters. But this new clientele scared away the high rollers and the casinos lost millions. So one day, "Baby strollers not allowed" signs popped up all over the strip and the kid-friendly venues disappeared. Overnight, Vegas again became "Sin City," the "What happens in Vegas, stays in Vegas" destination.

And it really is "Sin City." A couple of years ago I was gambling at the Paris, where I was staying, and went up to my room to get my reading glasses. No sooner did I enter my room when there was a loud pounding on the door. I called out, "Who's there?" A husky voice responded, "Hotel security! You got a hooker in there?" I indignantly replied, "No!" – So he threw one in!

Not long after the Paris Hotel opened on the Strip, my third (and final) wife, Fran, and I booked a room there. The first night, we decided to try their dinner buffet. There are two entrances to the buffet, one for high rollers and the other one for the rest of us peasants. While we were on the long peasant line, which had a 45-minute wait, one of the hostesses came out for a break. As she walked by, she glanced over at me, and then did a double-take. She looked absolutely stricken as she rushed over to Fran and me.

"Come with me, quickly! I'm so embarrassed! Please forgive me!" she gasped. She whisked us into the high roller entrance and whispered something to the maître d'. He glanced over to us, then smiled broadly and said, "Follow me." He led us inside the French village themed buffet and sat us down at a preferred table. "It is an honor to have you and your wife choose us for your dining pleasure. Be sure to tell your waiter your wine preference and he will bring you a bottle, on us, of course."

"Er, uh, thank you, but why are we receiving such preferential treatment?" I inquired.

The maître d' leaned in and said, in a soft voice, "It's not every day someone of your stature dines with us. Please let me know if you need anything, MR. SHATNER!"

I know I should have just gone along with it, but that's not who I am. "I'm not William Shatner!" I blurted out.

He smiled and whispered, conspiratorially, "I understand. You want to be left alone to enjoy your meal. Your secret is safe with me." And with that, he backed away.

I was sure there'd be a scene when I paid for the meal with the credit card that had my name on it, but the waiter informed me our meals had been comped. I gave the waiter and the maître d' generous tips, which still came out to much less than our meals would have been, and left quickly, certain that the cops would soon be after us.

The next time we ate there, months later, there was a new hostess, a new maître d', and no one rescued us from the peasant line.

Through the years, Fran and I have made this a little inside joke for ourselves. Once, I came home from work and Fran served me an elegant candlelit dinner in a revealing nightgown. And the best part was – she was the dessert! When I asked her what prompted her to spoil me in such a delightful manner, she answered, sexily, "It's not every night someone of your stature dines with me, Mr. Shatner!"

One time I went to see Elvis Presley at a dinner show at the old International Hotel, which later became the LV Hilton and is now the Westgate. Seated opposite from me were two young women in their late 20s. During the meal, they talked about their kids, school, their husbands, vacations – all the normal things married people discuss. Their husbands preferred to gamble in the casino to watching Elvis the Pelvis, but they didn't seem to mind.

Suddenly, the showroom went dark, the curtain opened, a powerful spotlight beamed its ray at the wings of the stage and then Elvis made his entrance. Dressed in a white, tight-fitting outfit, bedecked with glittering rhinestones, the King of Rock and Roll slithered and bumped his way to center stage, strumming his guitar and singing one of his first hits, "Hound Dog."

The two demure mommies who had sat rather quietly through dinner catapulted from their seats and began screaming, "We love you, Elvis!" They screamed throughout the entire song, eventually flinging their room keys and bras onstage!

This was one night when the women in the audience were a better show than the headliner.

The Pandemic all but closed Vegas for almost a year. But it was and will be again, the most exciting city in America. Vegas will bounce back and Mrs. Shatner and I will once more enjoy its shows, its decadence, its food, its glamour, and its slot machines.

You can bet on it.

JACK LEMMON

I played many rounds of golf at the Hillcrest Country Club with my father. I was always surprised to see so many stars who weren't members play golf there, like Dinah Shore and Sidney Poitier. But the most bizarre encounter I recall was with the acting legend Jack Lemmon.

Lemmon won awards for shows he did on Broadway and on television, but he is most remembered for his movie roles. He won a Best Supporting Actor Oscar for his work in "Mr. Roberts," and a Best Leading Actor trophy for "Save the Tiger." My favorite Lemmon films were "Some Like it Hot," "The Apartment" and "Grumpy Old Men." The last was one of eight pictures he made with his pal, Walter Matthau.

Being a golf nut, I watched Lemmon compete in the AT&T Pebble Beach Pro-Am golf tournament year after year. His quest to "make the cut" invariably ended badly. Millions of fans rooted him on, but his decades-long goal was never achieved.

One day my dad and I finished our round at Hillcrest. We were in the huge locker room, undressed and ready to go to the shower room, when we spotted Jack Lemmon across the aisle, seated on a bench, also naked.

Since Dad and I were both huge fans, we rushed over to him to chat. Lemmon was very gracious. He and his son, Chris, had just finished their round and he was about to shower, too. We must have chatted for ten minutes, all of us buck naked. Finally, we put towels around our privates and walked to the shower room.

A half hour later, Dad and I sat down at the dining room for lunch. As I was biting into a juicy burger, Jack Lemmon passed by and exchanged some pleasantries with Dad. Suddenly, Jack turned to me and scowled, "What's the matter, kid, you can't say hello?" Embarrassed, I blurted out, meekly, "I'm sorry, Mr. Lemmon. I didn't recognize you with your clothes on!"

Lemmon screamed with laughter. I gulped and took another bite of my burger, content with my accomplishment: I had made the great Jack Lemmon laugh.

JERRY LEWIS

When Joseph Levitch turned 13, his wealthy father decided to throw a grand Bar Mitzvah for his boy. He hired a young and rising comedian to perform at the pricy affair. That young comic was Murray Janofsky, nine years older than the Bar Mitzvah boy.

Ten years later, Murray Janofsky became Jan Murray and Joseph Levitch changed his name to Jerry Lewis.

They formed a friendship that lasted over 60 years.

Dad, with Buddy Hackett and Jerry Lewis

Jerry's partnership with the hilarious crooner Dean Martin catapulted them both to stardom, first in nightclubs, then on the silver screen. The Martin and Lewis films were numerous and extremely successful. After their split up, Jerry went it alone, achieving success not only as a comic, but as a singer, producer, actor and director. The great George Jessel once introduced Jerry to his radio show audience thusly, "My next guest is a comedian, an actor, a singer, a director, a producer, a fountain pen, a pup tent, a toilet plunger – he's everything. Ladies and gentlemen, please welcome the great Jerry Lewis!"

I saw a lot of Jerry growing up as he was a frequent guest at Dad's home as well as an occasional golfing buddy. And whenever Dad threw one of his parties at home, Jerry was always invited. I was lucky to be home to witness two monumental pranks that Jerry played at two of those parties.

Let me preface this by telling you about my father's home in Rye, New York. It had fourteen rooms on four acres of land. He turned the basement into a nightclub. It had several circular cabaret tables and a stage. On the stage was a piano, room for other musicians and a microphone. A spotlight could be worked from the back of the room. A motorized screen could be lowered like a curtain and movies could be shown on it from a small projection room across from the stage.

Through the years I was thrilled to watch his friends perform on that stage for the other show business guests. Steve Lawrence and Eydie Gorme frequently sang. Alan Sherman performed "Hello, Muddah,

Hello, Faddah" weeks before it became available to the public. Jules Styne played and sang the entire score of his masterpiece, "Gypsy" with all the guests singing along. Red Buttons tried out new material for his "Never Had a Dinner" routine. Sid Caesar would perform an entire sketch, playing all the characters, speaking nothing but gibberish, but able to convey the entire plot with his gestures and facial expressions.

There was always the promise of something great happening at one of Dad's parties, something that people could and would talk about for weeks. And Jerry Lewis was at the center of many of those happenings.

It was Sid Caesar's birthday and Dad threw him a party at the house. The basement club was filled with comedians and their spouses. There was great merriment, smoking and drinking going on when Milton Berle showed up, an hour late. He held a cigar box and yelled for everyone's attention. He had an announcement to make. The room hushed and Milton began.

"As you all know, the Cuban embargo has made it all but impossible to obtain Havanas, the best cigars on Earth. Through a connection, I was able to purchase this box of cigars for $6,000. Since they are so expensive, I will only smoke one of these babies on special occasions. Honoring Sid on his birthday is such an occasion."

With that, Milton took out one of his cigars and began explaining to everyone the painstaking process that was used to create such a fine cigar.

Needless to say, the party-goers were annoyed. Moments before, everyone was laughing and having a great time and now Berle was boring the hell out of the entire gathering about his stupid cigar.

Finally, Berle clipped off the end of the cigar, lit it, and took one long, luxurious drag. From out of nowhere, Jerry Lewis appeared with a pair of scissors, and snipped the cigar in two!

It was like someone had killed Milton's dog. While the guests gasped and then laughed uproariously, Berle became a wild man. He chased Jerry into the basement kitchen, where he found another pair of scissors. He caught up with Jerry, and cut off his expensive silk tie!

For the next twenty minutes, these two titans of comedy chased each other around the room, snipping off pieces of the other's clothing until both of them were literally wearing rags.

Sid Caesar, who rarely spoke in anything but doubletalk, blurted out, "Now THIS is a great birthday party!"

Jerry Lewis loved practical jokes. At a party at his house, he had hidden microphones placed in each room so that everything that anyone said could be recorded on tape recorders in his attic office. Through the evening, someone would comment about his poor taste in furniture, paintings, and decorating in general. Some even made caustic remarks about him. As all of his house guests sat down at his dining table for dinner, Jerry played back everything they had said about him over a loudspeaker! While some laughed, others understandably lost their appetites.

The year before Dad moved from his home in Rye to his new place in Beverly Hills, California, he threw another big party in his basement cabaret. It was an eclectic group of singers, actors (David Janssen was there), and comedians. This was still the 60s and everyone smoked. The room looked like a sauna.

Through the fog I heard Jerry Lewis approach my dad. "Hey, Jan, you got any Benson and Hedges cigarettes?"

Dad replied, "I have Kent, L & M, Newport, Marlboro, Salem and Winston. But I don't have Benson & Hedges."

"But I only smoke Benson & Hedges," Jerry whined.

"So you won't smoke for one night," Dad snorted. "It won't kill you." And with that, Dad moved away to talk to another guest.

I watched Jerry to see what his reaction would be to this rebuke. After a few seconds of thought, Jerry walked to the bottom of the stairs leading up to the main floor and called out to someone. After a moment, Jerry's chauffeur appeared. Jerry reached into his wallet and pulled out some bills. "Buy me some Benson & Hedges," he commanded his driver, "and don't bring me any change."

The chauffeur disappeared up the staircase and Jerry went back to the party. About 45 minutes later, the one small basement window, located at the top of the wall and the only window that opened to the outside world, was pushed open from the outside, and a coal chute was lowered into the room!

As everyone gasped at this spectacle, more than a thousand packs of Benson & Hedges poured down the chute and blanketed the floor!

"Hey, Jan," Jerry crowed, "you got Benson & Hedges now!"

Through the decades, Jerry Lewis raised more than a billion dollars for the Muscular Dystrophy Association at his annual telethon. Since Lewis was friends with so many celebrities and his telethon was seen by millions of viewers, the show was an important one for performers to be seen on. A star's appearance not only raised awareness and money for MDA, it also boosted the careers of those who performed – especially if they could somehow get Jerry to interact with them.

One night, at a dinner/roast that I attended, I found myself seated next to Shari Lewis. She had gained fame as a ventriloquist by using a sock puppet called Lamb Chop as her comedy foil. When she discovered that I was a comedy writer, she confided in me that she was going on Jerry's MDA telethon in a few days and wanted to do something special. She offered to hire me to write a back and forth comedy conversation between Lamb Chop and Jerry Lewis.

I wasn't really interested. At that point in my life I wrote scripts, not one-liners for dummies. "It only has to be a minute or two, something cute and funny. I'll give you a thousand bucks, cash, for a two-minute routine."

The reality was that the show I had been writing for had just been cancelled and I was waiting for my agent to find me another gig. So reluctantly, I took the assignment. My only stipulation was that she not tell anyone that I wrote her special material.

As I wrote the routine, I wondered how I'd gotten to this sorry state in my career. While others were writing plays and movies, I was writing jokes for a sock puppet!

I was watching TV the night of the telethon and saw Shari Lewis introduced. She crossed over to Jerry, held up Lamb Chop, and Jerry got big laughs literally "talking to the hand." The little routine went well. I got my thousand bucks and a nice letter of appreciation from Shari, and I never gave it a second thought. Truth be told, I was embarrassed to have taken the assignment and was glad no one knew about it.

A few years later, Jerry was over at Dad's house in Beverly Hills and I dropped in to say hi to the family. Dad bragged to Jerry about all the quality writing I was doing for "All in the Family" and other shows. Jerry pulled me aside and confided that he had to do a roast at the Friar's Club the next week. He wondered if I'd be open to writing some roast jokes for him.

I answered, "I'd love to, Jerry, but I'm a script writer, not a joke writer."

Jerry Lewis looked at me sternly. "Let me get this straight," he intoned, "for Jerry Lewis, an international star of nightclubs, stage, screen and movies, you won't write material, but you'll write jokes for LAMB CHOP?!"

As he did for his entire career, Jerry Lewis got the last laugh.

GARRY MARSHALL

Garry Marshall was a prolific writer, producer, director and creator. As an actor, I still remember his portrayal of Walter Harvey, the owner of the all-girl baseball league that flourished during World War II and was brought to the silver screen as "A League of their Own." In movies, he directed dozens of films, most notably "Pretty Woman," "Beaches," "The Runaway Bride," "The Princess Diaries," "The Flamingo Kid" and "Overboard." My contact with him was when he was the creator/producer of such television mega-hits as "Happy Days," "Laverne & Shirley" and "Mork & Mindy."

All three of those shows reached number one in the ratings. The networks kept begging him to create more hit shows for them, which he did. Unfortunately, one of them was a real clunker. It was called "Blansky's Beauties" and it starred a veteran comedic actress, Nancy Walker. The premise of the series was that Walker played a mother hen to several Las Vegas showgirls, keeping them virtuous, grounded and virginal. It was "The Facts of Life" meets "Sin City." The show lasted 13 episodes and I was on the writing staff.

Years earlier I had written an episode of "Happy Days" that Garry liked very much. He had wanted me to write more, but I was assigned to be the head writer for another show for big bucks, so I wasn't available. Later, when "Blansky's Beauties" was put on the schedule, Garry reached out and was delighted that I was available.

Garry was so busy keeping a close watch over all his on-air shows, it was hard to pin him down for script revisions. So the first time I found him alone in his office, I told him the writing staff couldn't find a "button" for a scene we were writing. A "button" is the finish to a scene. In a comedy, the button has to be funny or an "uh, oh" moment that propels the plot line along. The writing staff and I had tried more than a dozen buttons, but none of them seemed to work. I showed him the script we were working on and he read the scene.

"Warren," he announced, "what we need to end the scene is – a funny chair!"

I wasn't sure I heard him correctly. "A what?"

"We'll have the prop guys build a funny chair," he instructed. "And when Nancy sits in it – it'll collapse!"

I still wasn't sure he was serious. "That doesn't have anything to do with the plot," I protested.

"Who cares!?" he boomed. "She'll sit, the chair will fold up around her like a Venus flytrap, and everyone will laugh. Now THAT'S a button!"

Who was I to argue with the most successful producer in television? The chair was built, Nancy fell into it, the audience screamed with laughter, and we cut to the next scene.

A few years before "Blansky's Beauties," my agent got me in to "pitch" story ideas for the number one show in television, "Happy Days." I was a bit apprehensive. I had recently written for "All in the Family," and "Happy Days" was a much broader comedy, utilizing a lot of physical humor as opposed to character humor.

The thought occurred to me that "The Fonz," who had become the breakout star of the show, had a lot of rough edges. He never took off his leather motorcycle jacket and spoke in the colloquial vernacular of a typical Italian New Yorker. What if he met a stunning woman from high society, cultured, demure, rich and college educated? Could The Fonz win over such a magnificent creature?

In my pitch, I called the proposed episode "My Fair Fonzie." In it, Fonzie falls for such a beauty. She invites him for a chic dinner at her country club. I pictured everyone else in the cast prepping him for his "coming out" date. In other words, The Fonz was Eliza Doolittle and everyone else was Professor Higgins.

I got the assignment and Morgan Fairchild was cast as the society woman. The show's creator, Garry Marshall, invited me to the taping, which was performed in front of a live audience.

When the taping concluded, the audience filed out. Garry spotted me and asked me to stay. He wanted the cast to meet the "bright young man" who had written the episode. I was introduced to Tom Bosley and Marion Ross, who played the Cunninghams; Ron Howard, who played Richie Cunningham; Anson Williams, who portrayed Potsie; Donnie Most, who was Ralph Malph; Scott Baio, who played Chachi; and finally, I was introduced to Henry Winkler, The Fonz!

Garry said, "Henry, this is Warren Murray. He wrote this very funny show we did tonight." Henry stared at me and his eyes widened. He blurted out, "Warren Murray? Warren Murray?!!!"

I thought he was going to make a joke, like "Who the hell is Warren Murray?" Instead, he asked me, "Were you ever a counselor at Camp Winneshawauka?"

Note: It has been over forty years since this conversation took place, so I'm not completely positive that the camp Henry mentioned was Winneshawauka. It could have been any one of four summer camps where I was a counselor, but for the purposes of this account, I'll say it was Winneshawauka.

I was stunned. I HAD been a counselor there, actually a JUNIOR counselor (a J.C.) almost twenty years earlier; but how would he know that? After I nodded "yes" Henry told me this incredible story:

When Winkler was ten and I was 15, his parents placed him at Camp Winneshawauka, a sleepaway camp, for the entire summer. It was the first time he had ever been separated from them for such a long period of time and he was devastated. He cried, wouldn't eat, and refused to participate in any activities. He remembered vividly that the Junior Counselor in Bunk 2 spent a lot of time with him, calming him down and who finally coaxed him into giving camp a shot.

"Eventually," he continued, "I came around and had the best summer of my entire life. And I owed it all to my Junior Counselor. Warren – YOU were my counselor! You're my hero!"

With that, he gave me a hug. And, being in show business, I used this moment of hero worship to ask, "So, do you think I can parlay all this love into writing three more scripts?"

It turns out I never did. As I mentioned earlier, I was assigned full-time to another show and by the time it ended, "Happy Days" was off the air. The show ran for eleven seasons and did 255 episodes. But I'll always be proud of my tiny contribution.

Henry Winkler, by the way, has a reputation of being one of the truly "nice guys" in an egocentric business. Not only have I never heard anyone say a negative thing about him, but the people who have met and worked with him go out of their way to praise him as a true professional and a genuinely warm human being. I'm so glad I got a chance to meet him.

I didn't reconnect with Garry Marshall again until he asked me to write for "Blansky's Beauties." I recall another conversation I had with him. We were going over a script and during an impasse I asked him a question that all writers and would-be producers wanted to know.

"Garry, what's your secret? There are so many talented writers in this business, but only a chosen few ever reach the heights that you've attained. What's your secret?"

He looked up at me and smiled. "Warren, it's incredibly simple. I just have my characters say catch phrases that you can put on a t-shirt!"

"SIT ON IT!"

"AYYYYY!"

It was obviously a lot more than that, but for the rest of my career I tried to come up with a "Kiss My Grits!" or "Missed it by *that* much" saying that would catapult me into the upper echelon of the business. I never did, but for the rest of my writing career, whenever I got writer's block, I was always able to use Garry's trick to get over it – I had the prop guy build a funny chair!

MARRIAGE

Phyllis Diller said it best: "Anyone who claims marriage is a 50/50 proposition doesn't know the first thing about women or fractions."

I've been married three times, but that doesn't qualify me as an expert on marriage. On the contrary, it labels me as "the bad example." If you want to know what not to do to have a successful marriage, I'm your guy.

I often joke that my first two marriages ended in gunplay. That's not true, but both of those unions could be classified as civil wars.

I married my first wife when I was 21 and she was 18. Neither of us knew how to balance a bank statement or make a bed. But we were in LOVE. At least we thought we were in love. In actuality, we were in LUST. My father tried to convince me to wait to get married, but the more he persisted, the more I resisted. He even put together a new routine about youthful marriage in his act:

"In order to get a driver's license," he observed, "you have to pass a written test and a driver's test. In order to get a marriage license, you only have to pass a blood test! I think anyone under the age of 30 who wants to get married should have to pass a marriage test under actual battle conditions. Make the couple live together for six months in a one-room apartment, over a bowling alley, with a newborn infant who has colic, diaper rash and never sleeps. If that couple can complete six months of that still hugging, kissing and singing 'Zippity Doo Dah,' then, and only then should they get a marriage license!"

It was during this marriage that I saw my first flying saucer. Also, my first flying cup, blender and toaster! My wife was a thrower. Nothing in our apartment ever made it past the warranty period!

I discovered real quick that the heat of passion doesn't last forever when paying bills and having a kid insert themselves into married life. I remember asking my bride of a year why she didn't have orgasms anymore." I have plenty of orgasms," she responded. "Then why can't I hear them?" I asked. "Because," she explained, "You're never in the same room!"

This real life "Rocky Horror Show" got cancelled after five seasons, but two years later, I married again. As the great writer/philosopher Santana once said, "Those who don't learn from the mistakes of history are doomed to repeat them." That was, and still is, sage advice. Too bad I didn't heed it. I not only repeated the mistakes of my first marriage, I added new ones!

Once again I allowed my pecker to overrule my brain. I never looked beyond the pleasures of the moment to consider what the future held for this marriage. At first our love life was exciting. But two years into our union, my wife became what's usually referred to as "a screamer." Whenever we made love, she would shriek on top of her lungs, "GET OFF ME!"

I never minded her turning off the lights before we made love – it was the hiding that was so cruel!

I should have seen that as a sign, but I ignored it. And there were more signs. She didn't want me to smoke, so she made a deal with me. She bought me a pack of Marlboro's and told me I could only have one after we had sex. Twenty-one years later, when our marriage ended, I still had half a pack!

There were other signs that there was trouble in paradise. Whenever we went to sleep, she kept her elbow on my side, her knee on my side, her big toe on my side; the GOOD STUFF – she kept on HER side!

The only time she had sex with me was when she ran out of batteries!

Eventually, she placed a bunch of pillows in the center of our bed, effectively building a wall to keep out invaders. We were at war – and I was sleeping with the enemy!

There was another telling sign that I missed – everyday she made a "to-do" list – and I wasn't on it!

Just before we divorced, she protested that she still loved me. I told her, "If you really loved me, you would have married someone else!" She got angry and said, "You don't deserve a wife like me." I answered, "I've got kidney stones, and I don't deserve them either!" I had married her for her looks, but not the one she was giving me now!

Wife number two was a take-charge control freak as a business owner, a mother and a wife. When I feebly protested what she was saying or doing, she told me that she understood where I was coming from. From now on, she promised, she'd make the small, everyday decisions, and leave the big ones to me. So for more than two decades, she chose what we ate, where we vacationed, what cars to buy, and where we should live. The BIG decisions, like whether or not we should go to war with Iraq, she let me make! I was so henpecked, I cackled in my sleep!

The wonderful comic Norm Crosby told me this story about a henpecked husband:

A man dies and finds himself in a long line, behind dozens of men outside the Pearly Gates. Above the line is a huge sign that reads: HENPECKED HUSBANDS. He quickly decides that he's in the right line. As he's waiting his turn to meet St. Peter and enter Heaven, he notices another line. The sign above it says: MEN WHO DOMINATED THEIR WIVES. There's only one man in that line! As he gets closer, he realizes he knows this guy. It's Herbie, from where he worked. And the one thing he knows about Herbie is that he was the most henpecked husband who ever lived.

"Hey, Herbie!" he calls out. "What are you doing on THAT line?"

And Herbie answers, "My wife told me to stand here!"

My folks knew how whipped I had become, so a

year after my divorce, when I announced that I was marrying for a third time, my father gave me this advice, "Before you say 'I do,' tell your bride in no uncertain terms who the boss is in your marriage." So on my wedding day I walked up to my beautiful bride, Fran, looked her right in the eye, and proclaimed, "Honey – YOU'RE the boss!" And we've been happily married for 27 years!

Fran, and her ex-husband, Dave, were friends of mine and wife number two. We frequently ate out together, even went on trips together. So when both of our marriages ended, we first got together to commiserate, as friends. It wasn't that big of a leap before we became romantically involved. I can tell you all that dating someone you've known for 14 years has its advantages.

I was already over 50, so doing the whole singles scene again was pretty scary for me. I mean, I still dipped when I danced! Fran knew me, my past, and most of my eccentricities. I didn't have to pretend to be a CIA agent or whisper to her, "Don't move your foot. I seem to have dropped my Congressional Medal of Honor on the floor and I don't want you to step on it!"

We got married in the banquet room of the Los Robles Golf Course, in Thousand Oaks, California. While we were exchanging our vows, we could hear a loudspeaker outside the room announcing, "On the first tee, the Johnson foursome!" I leaned into the rabbi who was presiding over our nuptials and whispered, "Could you speed this up? I have a tee time in half an hour!"

Fran and me at our wedding

I love watching sports. Fran has a way of entering the room and begin talking to me at the most crucial moment of whatever game I'm watching. It's bad enough that she's a "low-talker," like the woman on "Seinfeld." Even when she has my full attention, it's sometimes difficult to hear what she's saying. So with bases loaded, two out in the ninth and a full count, I often don't even know she's talking to me. Then, suddenly, in a much louder voice, she says, sternly, "Well, do you agree with me or not?"

This, I hear. Instantly, I know I'm in big trouble. I have no idea what she's talking about, but I know she expects an answer from me. If I say "yes," I could, like Jerry Seinfeld, end up wearing a puffy shirt! If I say "No," I know she'll ask me "Why not?" I could admit I wasn't paying attention to her because of the game I was watching. But that would be met with,

Fran and me in front of the Sydney Opera House

"So what are you saying? Baseball is more important than I am?" More often than not, I fall back on my last line of defense – I fake a heart attack!

Fran and I have been to all 50 states and have travelled all over the world.

We had to cancel three wonderful trips when the pandemic hit, and we've been basically joined at the hip at home for over a year, waiting for life to reopen. The fact that we've spent all this time together for such a long time – without killing each other – speaks volumes about the durability of our marriage.

When Fran and I first married, we ate out all the time. She rarely did any cooking. I used to joke that the inside of the oven had cobwebs!

I told everyone that when Fran cooked for the family, we prayed AFTER the meal!

She thought the chicken was done when the feathers turned black!

She once made alphabet soup and it spelled "UGH!"

She made me frozen dinners before there was TV!

She makes very strong coffee. This morning I was stirring and I bent the spoon!

She thinks soy sauce means "I am sauce!"

When I wrote for the TV series "Alice," I used to make all these jokes about Mel's cooking in his diner. The cast never knew I was really writing about Fran's cooking! Or so I thought, until the pandemic hit. Fran has cooked dinner almost every night for over a year – and she's a terrific cook! I can't wait for dinner anymore. "Don't get used to it," she recently told me. "I hate to cook. When restaurants reopen, I'm never cooking again!" Is it selfish of me to hope the pandemic continues?

The differences between Fran and my first two spouses is like night and day. The first two were loud and bossy. Fran never tells me what to do – she just points!

I mean it. If something is bothering her, she keeps it to herself. Fran suffers in silence louder than anyone I know!

Fran and me

I've learned the one immutable law of marriage – there's only one way to handle a woman – and no one knows what it is!

Someone once said, "It's better to have loved and lost than never to have loved at all." After 27 happy years with my Fran, I'd like to amend that saying:

"It's better to have loved and won – much better!"

JACKIE MASON

I've always been a fan of Jackie Mason. You may remember him from TV and film, or as a stand-up comedian. But I loved his one-man stage shows like "The World, According to Me," "Jackie Mason, Freshly Squeezed" and "The Ultimate Jew."

His routines comparing gentiles to Jews are classics. "After my show, gentiles will say 'Want a drink?' 'Let's have a drink.' The Jews will say, 'Have you eaten yet? Let's have some cake!'"

He once observed, "Gentiles leave and never say goodbye; Jews say goodbye and never leave!"

Not wanting to offend non-Jews in his audience, he would proclaim, "Gentiles are good people. Gentiles are fine people." Then he'd peer into the audience and point at someone sitting in the front row. "Not YOU, sir, but most!"

My father was good friends with Jackie. Mason always asked Dad not to throw away any of his monogrammed shirts, since they both had the same initials. Dad was 6' 2" and Jackie was about 5' 7". "My shirt sleeves will hang over you so much, you'll look like a gorilla," Dad would tell him. Jackie would shrug and tell him he'd wash the shirts in hot water and run them through the dryer until they shrunk down to his size.

I once ran into Jackie when he was performing at the

Fontainebleau Hotel in Miami Beach. I introduced myself and he gave me a hug. I told him how glad I was to see him performing, since I hadn't seen him for a while. He said, "I owe it all to my new agent. I just signed with the William Morris Agency. They have offices in Los Angeles, New York, London and Paris. Now when I'm out of work, I'm out of work all over the world!"

He then confided, "To tell you the truth, I don't have to work at all. I have enough money to last me the rest of my life." I said, "Terrific." "Unless," he added, "I buy something."

When Mason turned 90, he was asked what he does to stay healthy. He answered, "At 90, it's no longer a question of staying healthy. It's a question of finding a sickness I like!"

Jackie Mason is part of that wonderful generation of comics who commented about the human condition in recognizable, clean and truly funny monologues. We need more like him today.

MOVIES

I love watching movies, especially ones that make me laugh. I can't understand why comedies, for the most part, are always overlooked during Oscar season. I guess the snooty judges don't find them highbrow enough. Still, comedies rank as some of the best written, most enjoyable films I've ever seen. They include "A Fish Called Wanda," "50 First Dates," "Groundhog Day," "Analyze This," "City Slickers," "When Harry Met Sally," "Young Frankenstein" and so many others. They were well-written, well-acted, and moved us to laugh and escape from the miseries of everyday life, which is the purpose of motion pictures.

Don't get me wrong, I love a great drama. Who wouldn't be moved by "Life Is Beautiful," "The Lion in Winter" or any film ever directed by Alfred Hitchcock? But this book isn't called "Dramatic Side Up," so I shall focus on comedic movies.

What separates a blockbuster script from one that's not even made? I think TITLES have something to do with that. Take, for instance, several film scripts that I wrote "on spec" that never got made: "Apocalypse Soon," "Down and Out in Beverly Sills" and "Saving Ryan's Privates." See, it was the titles that doomed my projects!

I'm always amused by the rating system they use for movies to warn moviegoers of possible objectionable content. So let me clarify it for you. In a G-rated movie, the hero gets the girl. In an X-rated film, EVERYBODY gets the girl!

The ratings seem to send mixed signals. If, in a film, a man kisses a woman's bare breast, the movie is rated X. But if he cuts off her breast with a chainsaw – then it's an R!

Some of those massacre films are so bloody, they're rated Type A!

Today, what used to be rated X is considered ho-hum. In fact, there's so much nudity in films this year, the Oscar for Best Costume Design will probably go to a dermatologist!

In the old days, actresses used to play parts – now they reveal them!

The truth is that not all motion pictures are worth seeing. If a studio can hit a home run with one out of every five films it puts out, they'll make a profit. Which means there are a lot of clunkers out there for you to waste your money on. I mean, I hate it when I go to the movies and people wait in long lines to get out! I remember when I lived back east, I went to a drive-in and the movie was so terrible, people asked for their gas back!

The point of all this is that movies are a part of all our lives. We may love them or hate them, but we can't live without them. And despite the low percentage of success, I'll continue to dish out my big bucks in the hope that I'll be witness to a new movie classic. Especially if it's funny.

NATHAN'S HOT DOGS

Brooklyn in the 1950s was noted nationwide for its Dodgers baseball team, Coney Island and Nathan's Hot Dogs. Its one stand in Coney Island opened in 1916 and sold its dog for ten cents. It's rumored that the thin pork sausage was sold inside a bun so the owners wouldn't have to lay out money for cutlery or plates.

By 1950, Nathan's hot dogs were the gold standard, not only for Brooklynites, but for all New Yorkers. When I moved to California in 1967, one of the things I missed most about my childhood was a Nathan's hot dog. It was still only sold in that one stand in Coney Island. Expansion to seemingly every food court and supermarket in America didn't occur until years later.

It should be noted that armies of comedians and show business performers moved to California in the 60s, as the television and motion picture industries shifted from New York to the West Coast. Even the Dodgers moved to California. The only thing that didn't move west was Nathan's hot dogs.

A few months after I moved to California, my father asked me if I had a tuxedo. I didn't and he told me to rent one. I was very excited. Maybe he was taking me to a big movie premiere, or an awards show. My excitement dwindled rapidly when he told me we were invited to a formal dinner party at his friend Paul Burke's home in Beverly Hills.

A prolific television and motion picture actor, Burke was at the top of his career in the 60s, starring in two hit TV series on ABC, "Naked City" and "12 O'Clock High." Dad assured me that I would love the evening, as there would be many stars of movies and TV over for dinner at Burke's mansion.

We arrived, and present was a "Who's Who" of comedy and acting, all dressed stylishly. Waiters scampered about with trays of hors d'oeuvres and drinks. After a while, we were all ushered into the huge formal dining room, which was set with elegant silverware and china. As the guests waited with breathless anticipation for what they were sure would be a gastronomical extravaganza, Burke gave a signal and a dozen waiters entered the banquet room carrying covered chafing dishes.

The waiters set their food down on the table and with a flourish, removed the tops of all the chafing dishes, revealing – Nathan's hot dogs!

It was at that moment that I realized that everyone invited to that dinner was a transplanted New Yorker! Everyone present had secretly bemoaned the fact that they hadn't had a great hot dog since they moved to California.

On the table were other dishes filled with relish, onions, sauerkraut, buns – everything one needed to consume the treasured and rare hot dogs. As refined and cultured as the show business royalty appeared that night, they attacked those hot dogs in a feeding frenzy reminiscent of a piranha devouring a cow!

Today, of course, you can get a Nathan's hot dog everywhere, but Burke had flown in more than 100 frozen Nathan's hot dogs – and for a few enchanted moments, we were all back in Coney Island, reliving our childhoods.

OCCUPATIONS

When I was growing up, there was a popular game show on TV called "What's My Line?" On every show there were three contestants, and panelists each asked ten questions which could be answered by a "yes" or a "no" in an attempt to guess what the contestant did for a living. I was always amazed at how many occupations there were.

My father illustrates this perfectly. You might remember him as comedian Jan Murray. But he never graduated from high school because he had to find a job to help support his family during the Great Depression. His job? He worked in a doll factory, screwing the heads onto the dolls! Think of how much he would've won on "What's My Line?"

Before I became a television comedy writer, producer, network executive and teacher, I had a lot of part-time summer jobs. I was a summer camp counselor, an archery instructor, I sold "no solicitation" signs door-to-door, and was even a lifeguard in a car wash! In college I was into public service. I used to provide temporary relief for nymphomaniacs!

Okay, the last three were jokes, but I always dreamed of coming up with a gimmick that could make me a young millionaire. One scheme involved me owning and operating a chain of drive-thru confessionals! The church was understandably cool to the idea.

Before my mom, Pearl (Dad's first wife), gave up

show business to raise me, she was a talented singer who once won a Major Bowes Talent Show radio contest. That show was the forerunner of "Star Search," "American Idol," "America's Got Talent" and all the other talent shows that serve as the launching pad for so many careers.

My wife and I have large families representing a wide spectrum of occupations. My wife's nephew, Jeff, is our accountant. He's well-respected in his field. He wrote the book on Accounts Deceivable!

The IRS recently named a tax loophole after him!

The way he cooks the books ten people could eat!

He once told me I could claim a deduction for my parrot – if I could teach it to only talk business!

Unable to reconcile my bank statement, I asked him to check my balance – so he pushed me!

Even though he's a relative, I was stunned at the bill he sent me after the last tax season. When I complained, he said, "You're such an ingrate. And to think I named my yacht after you!"

He recently went into business with Toyota. They make the cars – he makes the license plates!

There's also a dentist in my family, my dad's cousin, Arnold. After many years, he went into semi-retirement, practicing only from his houseboat at Marina Del Rey. He put out a shingle that read, "Offshore Drilling!"

Arnold once told the family a story about one of his patients. He was a Maharishi. He insisted that all the work on his crown be done without painkillers. When he asked his patient if he was sure he didn't want some Novocain, the Maharishi answered, "I'm sure. I wish to transcend dental medication!" It appears everyone in the family was a comedian.

I also have a lawyer in my family. Gary is really brilliant. I've watched him in court several times. He invented a strategy that never fails. He keeps giving his closing argument until the Statute of Limitations runs out!

He truly believes that a man is innocent until proven broke!

One of his clients was charged with felony sodomy. Gary got his case reduced to a misdemeanor – following too closely!

One of his clients was convicted of murder, but Gary cleverly got the guy a reduction – in voltage!

I once got sued and I asked him how I should plead. He said, "On your knees!"

I shouldn't make fun of his profession. After all, lawyers are experts on justice, the same way hookers are experts on love!

He's living proof that 99% of lawyers give the rest a bad name!

Only kidding. Gary is an entertainment lawyer and well-respected by his cell-mates!

Red Buttons once told me this story about a lawyer:

A lawyer and the Pope both pass away at the same time and find themselves in front of the Pearly Gates. St. Peter tells both of them that they have been approved to spend eternity in Heaven and will show them where they will reside until the end of time. St. Peter takes the lawyer to a huge castle, filled with servants who will wait on him hand and foot. The castle has an 18-hole golf course and a sparkling lake. And he gets to drive around Heaven in a Rolls Royce Corniche convertible. The lawyer is thrilled and St. Peter takes the Pope to his eternal domain. It is a ten-story tenement. The Pope's apartment is on the top floor. There is no elevator and the Pontiff has to share a bathroom with all the other tenants on his floor. The Pope is understandably upset. "There has to be some mistake," he cries. "I spent my entire life spreading God's word and you give that guy a castle and me a run-down apartment?" St. Peter explains, "I can understand your consternation, your Holiness, but you see, it's like this – you're our 230th Pope – but he's our first lawyer!"

My family tree represents a cross-section of careers and jobs. For many years, my wife, Fran, was a game show question writer for several shows, which made her a walking encyclopedia of trivia. To this day, when we're having dinner and I ask her for "seconds," she invariably replies, "For seconds, what's the capital of Maine?" If I don't answer correctly, (Augusta) I get NOTHING! Some nights, I don't even get FIRSTS!

Other family members include teachers, school administrators, a doctor, an entertainment lawyer, two paralegals, accountants, an opera singer, a game show writer, a real estate agent, an aerospace engineer, a tech start-up entrepreneur, a fund raiser, a nurse and even a plumber – who, luckily, is always at our disposal. There are thousands of occupations and thankfully, all of them can be relished and savored FUNNY SIDE UP.

OLD AGE

When I was a child, I would hear family members cry and moan over the passing of someone they knew in their 60s. To a ten-year-old, that seemed ancient. I reasoned that a 60-year-old had lived a full life, so why was everyone carrying on so much?

Now that I'm 79, I'll read an obituary about someone who died at 92 and think to myself, "That poor man, cut down in his prime!"

There's an old saying that "old age is anyone 20 years older than I am." The truth, though, is that at 79, I'm the one who's 20 years older than most everyone else.

How can I convince myself I still have many years ahead of me when all I have to do is look in a mirror. The bags under my eyes are so large, airlines charge me $25 apiece for them! My face has so many wrinkles, it could hold six days' rain! I'm starting to look like a Shar Pei puppy!

I'm three inches shorter than I was 20 years ago and I keep answering the phone all day because the ringing in my ears never stops!

Woody Allen once remarked, "I want to live forever. So far, so good!" Even though I diet and exercise regularly, I know I'm sliding down the razor blade of life. The great philosopher, Steven Wright, put it best, "Every day I beat my previous record for the number of consecutive days I've stayed alive!"

So rather than moan "Why me?" I've chosen to look at the funny side of growing old. As each of my older relatives and friends have had birthdays and anniversaries, they've called on me to "roast" them. I have found that a little "longevity levity" beats anguish and remorse anytime.

In these roasts, I created many of the lines myself. Others, I either remembered or blatantly stole from comedians and cave drawings. The great Bob Hope kept a file of thousands of pages of jokes. When he was asked to perform, he and his writers would go through his files and change, bend, shape, elaborate and embellish the original joke to fit the occasion or audience he was performing for.

And so, instead of bemoaning how yucky it is to grow old, I have decided to pass on some of my favorite Old Age jokes that I've used to roast my loved ones through the years. Undoubtedly, you've heard many of them, and if you're reading this in your youth, you may not even understand the humor – until all the things I talk about begin to happen to you.

So under the heading YSO (You're So Old), here is how old farts like me joke about ourselves:

YSO – People call you at 7 p.m. and ask, "Did I wake you?"

YSO – In a hostage situation, you're likely to be

released first!

YSO – You and your spouse go out once a week and paint the town grey!

YSO – You actually enjoy hearing about other people's operations!

YSO – Your joints forecast the weather better than the National Weather Service!

YSO – You shake the last drop – and dust comes out!

YSO - You start every sentence with, "Nowadays ..."

YSO – You look both ways before crossing a room!

YSO – Your childhood toys are now in museums!

YSO – All your favorite movies are now becoming colorized!

YSO – Your favorite color is beige!

YSO – Your measurements are small, medium and large – in that order!

YSO – Whenever you stop to think – you forget to start again!

YSO – You remember what the best thing was BEFORE sliced bread!

YSO – Your knees buckle – but your belt won't!

YSO – Your birthstone is lava!

YSO – Your blood type has been discontinued!

YSO – "The other day" means any time between yesterday and 20 years ago!

YSO – It's hard for you to respect your elders – because you can't find any!

YSO – People stand around your birthday cake just to keep warm!

YSO – All the numbers in your Little Black Book are doctors!

YSO – Your first job was parking covered wagons!

YSO – You can run like the winded!

YSO – You've stopped buying green bananas!

YSO – Your Social Security Number is 2!

YSO – You've gone from Acid Rock to Acid Reflux!

YSO – "Getting Lucky" means finding your car in the parking lot!

YSO – When Cain slew Abel – you sat on the jury!

YSO – You have an autographed Bible!

YSO – An "all-nighter" means not getting up to use the bathroom!

YSO – You remember when the wonder drug was leeches!

YSO – You knew Michelangelo when he only did walls!

YSO – You recall when sex was dirty and the air was clean!

YSO – Your doctor tells you to slow down instead of the police!

YSO – You no longer have to worry about peer pressure!

YSO – You used to want a BMW, but now you don't care about the "W"!

YSO – Your birthday candles cost more than the cake!

YSO – Your grandkids play connect-the-dots on your liver spots!

YSO – You're actually starting to like accordion music!

YSO – You consider "happy hour" the time you nap!

YSO – You put tenderizer on your Cream of Wheat!

YSO – When you went to school, the Revolutionary War was called "the News!"

YSO – You can actually spell "gastroenterologist!"

YSO – You don't lie about your age – you brag about it!

YSO – Everything of yours is starting to wear out, fall out or spread out!

YSO – You're starting to remember things that never happened!

YSO – The first seder you went to WAS the first seder!

YSO – Whenever you get an idea, a CANDLE appears over your head!

These are just some of the silly observations we old folks make about our "condition." Some of them aren't so funny anymore because they hit too close to home. I mean, the last time I ate breakfast out at a deli, I ordered a three-minute egg – and they asked me to pay in advance!

Boy Scouts keep walking me across the street – even when I don't want to go!

The other day I saw a really old person – and I realized I went to school with him!

I'm freaking out about turning 80 and my friends try

to console me by saying, "Don't worry, 80 is the new 60." Maybe, but what's also true is that 9 P.M. is the new Midnight!

Sometimes I feel so ancient, I get the urge to put an "Out of Order" sticker on my forehead and call it a day. But then I say to myself, "Hey, I may not be that athletic or good looking or smart or talented..." I forgot where I was going with this. Which illustrates the point perfectly that senility has been a smooth transition for me!

Okay, so I may not look as good as I used to, but the people I want to look good for can't see as well as they used to, either!

I read an article the other day that said that seniors are the largest carriers of AIDS. It may be true – Hearing aids, First aids, Rolaids...

A lot of people my age wish they were young again. I guess that would be nice, but I'm actually okay with where I am in life. At least we old codgers can remember what it was like to be young. Young people can only GUESS what it's like to be old. And while it's true that many of us can't hear – it's also true that many young people can't listen. I try really hard not to dwell on the good old days. Instead, I'm trying to create some good NEW days.

Still, like all seniors, I tend to reflect on my life and ask myself what I've learned in my 79 years. So here are some of my insights about old age:

I never eat "health foods" – at my age, I need all the preservatives I can get!

Age is a matter of mind over matter – if you don't mind, it doesn't matter!

Age gets better with wine!

I'm almost at the age when I'm going to leave little bags of snacks on the floor all over the house – in case I fall down and can't get up!

I never worry about senility. When it hits me – I won't remember!

I've learned to not do something permanently stupid because I'm temporarily upset.

I now realize that even though my hearing is going and my eyesight is going, and my memory is going – I'm still going, too.

I've come to the conclusion that being over the hill is better than being under it.

And finally, if things get better with age – I'm pretty close to magnificent!

Me – the old and magnificent version

PROFESSORS

In September of 1959, at the age of 17, I began my undergraduate studies at New York University. I was really looking forward to being taught by professors, who I considered to be at the top of the educational totem pole. I secretly wanted to be a professor. The idea of wearing a corduroy jacket with leather elbow patches while sucking on a pipe was my idea of nirvana.

My worship of professors eroded through the four years I attended NYU. I realized that although they were knowledgeable in their fields, many of them were conceited, boring and made no effort to "connect" with their students. Just like teachers in every grade I had passed through, some inspired me to think, do research or take some action for the betterment of mankind. Others made me want to donate my tuition to Yawn research.

I had a history professor, Dr. Olson, who read each lecture from ancient parchment paper in a monotone voice. The old man never looked up, not even once, during the entire semester I sat in his lecture hall. He didn't teach history – he remembered it!

One character I vividly remember was named Gaynor Braddish. He had bright red hair, hence his nickname – Braddish the Radish! Braddish had a nasty habit of coming into the classroom late every day. NYU had a rule that if a professor didn't show up within 10 minutes of its scheduled start, the class was cancelled for that day and all the students could leave. Braddish would enter the room in the ninth minute, just as all of us were packing up our books and preparing to leave.

We wanted to teach him a lesson, so one day, while we were waiting for his arrival, we took the lectern he always stood behind to deliver his lectures, and put it out on the fire escape outside the large window in our room. At the nine-and-a-half-minute mark, Braddish entered the room. Without hesitating, or reacting in any way, he strode to the window, climbed through it – and delivered the entire lecture from the fire escape!

Another notable faculty member was Professor Tan. He was an exchange professor from China who was brought in to lecture us on Chinese history. There was no textbook for Chinese history, so we had to write down whatever he said that we thought might show up on his exam. This was no easy task, since Professor Tan had a very thick accent.

He began, "Many people believe the first Homo Sapiens appeared in Africa, but this is not so. They began in China. We know this from traces of cell and bung that have been found by archaeologists."

I dutifully wrote "cell" and "bung" in my notebook, waiting for him to explain what they were. He lectured for a full hour and never referred to those terms again. When the bell rang, I had to leave quickly because my next class was at the other end of the campus.

A week later, we had our first test. Although I got an "A," I did miss one question. It was, "How do we know that Homo Sapiens originated in China?" I had written, quite confidently, "Because archaeologists have found traces of cell and bung." When I showed Professor Tan my paper, he stared at my answer and asked, "What is this cell and bung?" I replied I had no idea. "This is what I wrote in my notes from your lecture." He stared at me incredulously. "There's no such thing as cell and bung," he insisted. "Then how do we know Homo Sapiens began in China?" I persisted. Professor Tan walked to the blackboard, chalk in hand, and answered, "Because archaeologists found traces of ... (and he wrote on the board) SHELL and BONE!

NYU loved to have visiting professors. My favorite was a Professor Wainwright, from just outside London. He had a deep voice, pronounced every syllable of every word, and could have easily replaced Rex Harrison on Broadway as Henry Higgins in "My Fair Lady."

This was an English Literature class, and Wainwright was considered a major authority on the works of Geoffrey Chaucer, having just written a 900-page book on the English author. His book was required reading in his class and could be used effectively as a substitute for chloroform.

Wainwright had a tic when he spoke. He was constantly lifting up his chin and moving it from side to side as though his collar was too tight. And each time he made that movement, he emitted an audible CLICK sound from deep in his throat. Since he delivered his lesson in the largest lecture hall on campus, he spoke into a microphone, which magnified the CLICK sound for the close to 500 students to hear. Miriam Makeba, who introduced "The Click Song" on a Harry Belafonte record album, would have been proud of Wainwright's prolific clicking.

I had an idea. Being short of cash, I devised a contest. For one dollar, a student in this class could bet on how many clicks Wainwright would emit during any given lecture. They would write their name and their guess on the paper and give it to me with their dollar. I would keep score and be the only judge. The contest would end when the bell rang, ending the lecture. This was important, since Wainright often droned on well past the bell, even as the room was emptying out. If more than one student picked the exact number, they'd split the pot. What I didn't tell them was that I skimmed 20% from the pot, which I took before I gave the winner(s) the rest. As the contest gained participants, I made out very well.

The lecture hall was always full and the bettors often kept their own tallies, so as the lecture neared an end, and Wainwright's clicks approached the number students had written on their betting slips, a loud murmur began to build in the room. "C'mon, baby, just three more!" CLICK. "Two! C'mon, two." CLICK. "Yeah! One more and I win!" CLICK. "I won! I won!" CLICK CLICK CLICK! "Ahhh, shit!"

The bell would ring amidst cheers, boos and curses. Wainwright could never understand why there was always so much bedlam going on towards the end of all his lectures. Surprisingly, I got an A in the class, even though I never listened to anything he said except for his CLICKS, -- which is amazing, since Chaucer made less sense to me than cell and bung!

RELIGION

G. K. Chesterton once observed, "It is the test of a good religion if you can joke about it." Some modern religions will behead you if you joke about them, or fly airplanes into buildings if you satirize their beliefs in any way, so those religions may not pass the test.

My mom and dad were Jewish, so I, without being consulted, became one at the moment of birth. My parents didn't observe most of the Jewish rituals. We didn't go to services or keep a kosher home. My grandmother, who lived with us for most of my life, had lots of Yiddish expressions. One was "Gay cockin offin yom," which, loosely translated means "Go take a crap in the ocean!" She also had another expression which I can't recall in Yiddish, but means, "You should swallow a trolley bell, and the conductor should ring it in your stomach every ten minutes!"

My father's parents prayed every morning and attended services regularly. But when Dad married Toni Kelly, a Southern Baptist, he scaled down his religious participation to the High Holidays (Rosh Hashanah and Yom Kippur) and to presiding over the family seders on Passover.

Dad threw two seders every year. The first was for family and adhered closely to the prayers, readings and rituals of the dinner. The second seder was for his comedian and show business friends and their spouses! Despite Dad's efforts to maintain a sense of solemnity and decorum, the dinner usually disintegrated into chaos and hilarity in short order. When Steve Lawrence and Eydie Gorme attended, Dad would say, "Tonight we're going to sing the hymn Chad Gadya to the tune of 'Blame It on the Bossa Nova!"

When Uncle Miltie (Berle) was there, he would finish off an entire decanter of Manischewitz before the first prayer for the drinking of the wine!

Sid Caesar, when asked to read from the Haggadah (prayer book) would instead unleash a hilarious stream of Jewish-sounding double-talk!

Mel Brooks once attended with his wife, Anne Bancroft. When it ended, I asked him how he enjoyed the meal. A normal person would have answered, "It was delicious." But Mel's response was, "My tongue is throwing a party for my mouth!"

The seder table was always put together by Toni's mother, Bertie, who was born and raised in Montezuma, Georgia. If left to her own devices, she would have fried everything on the table, including the gefilte fish! Luckily, Dad's rabbi instructed her on what to put out, like the haroset, bitter herbs and matzo. Bertie had no idea that the matzo signified the unleavened bread Moses and his followers ate as they wandered through the desert for 40 years, trying to escape Egyptian slavery. So when she put together her first seder table, she suddenly turned to me with a stricken look on her face and cried, "Your father's going to kill me – I forgot the dinner rolls!"

Dad always joked about his lack of religiosity. He would say, "My temple is so reform, they close for the High Holidays!" "I belong to the most reform temple in California – Temple Beth Christ!" He told people that Sammy Davis, Jr., who converted to Judaism, started a temple for Black people who also converted. "It's called, "Temple Beth You is my Woman Now!" And he would add, "It's right across the street from Temple Bet Midler!"

With a Baptist wife, the Murray family celebrated both Hannukah and Christmas. The entire month of December was a festival of greed. When I asked Dad how he could celebrate Christmas and call himself a Jew, he replied, "In this family, we celebrate any holiday that involves food and gifts!"

I was Bar Mitzvahed, which was very exciting for me because everyone told me it meant that "Today, I am a man!" But that night, my mom told me to take out the trash and finish my homework or I'd be grounded. My manhood lasted less than a day!

In my studies for my Bar Mitzvah, I was taught how to read Hebrew, but never what any of the words and prayers meant. All I really learned about God was that He doesn't eat pork – and He's allergic to shellfish!

I have a problem with the whole notion of a Supreme Being who created everything, looks out for us and who will embrace us for all eternity after we die. After all, we can't see, hear, feel, touch or taste God.

To believe in such a being requires FAITH, based on – faith! I used to have that kind of faith in Santa Claus and the Tooth Fairy – and that faith didn't turn out so great. Still, I'm secretly jealous of people who have that faith. They go through life with a peace, a serenity, a glow, a faraway look that only True Believers and people wearing MAGA hats possess.

Shecky Green told this story about faith:

A man accidently drives off the top of a cliff. On the way down, he leaps from the car, reaches out and grabs the one small branch jutting out from the mountain. He watches in horror as the car smashes into the rocks below and erupts in a fireball. He calls up, "CAN ANYONE HEAR ME?" There's a clap of thunder and a voice from the sky answers: "I hear you, my child!" The man is incredulous. "God? Is that you?" The voice answers, "It is I!" The man can't believe his good luck. "I thought I was doomed, but, can you help me?" God responds, "Of course I can help you, but only if you have absolute faith in me. Do you believe in me?" "Oh, yes, I believe! I believe!" the man cries out. The voice instructs, "In that case, all you have to do is let go of the branch – and I'll take care of the rest!" The man thinks for a few seconds, then yells on top of his lungs, "Can anyone ELSE hear me?!"

Comedian Morey Amsterdam once gave me his take on Faith:

A young Protestant from the Midwest visited the

Wailing Wall in Jerusalem and saw a very old Jewish man praying loudly and woefully. The young man interrupted the prayer. "Excuse me, sir, but I can't help noticing you crying out. Are you in pain?" The old man answered, "I'm not crying, I'm praying to God that he should put an end to all suffering, anger, bigotry, starvation and war." The young man observed, "That's a very noble sentiment. Do you pray here often? The old man retorted, "I've come here every day for 62 years and each day I pray that God will put an end to all the misery there is in this world." The young man was awed. "Sixty-two years! Wow! Tell me, old man, do you think all your praying is doing any good? The old man thought for a moment and answered, "Nahhhh – it's like talking to a wall!

I find it strange that the same arguments put forward to "prove" the existence of a single, all-seeing, all-knowing God can be used to prove the existence of many Gods. Why can't there be a God of rain, snow, grass, Hula Hoops and Ding Dongs? And why is God a male? Whether there is one God or many, why can't He or They be female? Maybe God is a dog. "Dog" is "God," backwards. Coincidence?

True Believers now hate me. How dare I question their faith? They tell me I'm going to burn in Hell. Well, maybe. I'll believe it when I see it. In the meantime, I can't conceive it's possible to ever prove the existence of a Supreme Being. Because of that, I've been labeled by some as an Agnostic. I once told my next door neighbor that I was an Agnostic – and that night he burned a question mark on my front lawn!

Since I question if there even is a Supreme Being, some people call me an Atheist. I've heard all the jokes about Atheists. "Atheists have no holidays," "Atheists have no invisible means of support," etc. Telling people I'm an Atheist gets me such negative responses, I now tell them I'm a Seventh Day Absentist!"

Whether from God or evolution, we all possess brains and free will. We can decide for ourselves whether to pursue good or evil, brotherhood or racism, intelligence or stupidity. As for me, I've chosen to devote my life pursuing the funny side of everything – even a touchy subject like religion.

Thank God I'm an Atheist!

DON RICKLES

Don Rickles had a long and successful career as an "insult" comic. It became a badge of honor to brag to everyone that you had been picked on by Rickles. Stars felt slighted if they attended Don's show and he didn't go after them.

One night, when Don was young and still single, he was having dinner with his date at his favorite restaurant when he spied Frank Sinatra across the room. Rickles excused himself and went to Sinatra's table. "Frank," he said, "I'd love it if you could drop by my table and say hello to me. My date's a big fan and it would really build me up in her eyes if she saw you knew me." Frank agreed and Rickles went back to his table. A few minutes later, Frank Sinatra walked over to Don's table and said, "Hi, Don. Good to see you." Rickles looked up and barked in disgust, "Not now, Frank! Can't you see I'm eating?!"

When Rickles was first introduced to Earnest Borgnine, he commented, "Oh my God, look at you! Was anyone else hurt in the accident?!"

When he spotted Bob Hope in his audience, Don snickered, "Bob is so popular, when he was in Vietnam they were shooting at him from both sides!"

To Yul Brenner, he sneered, "Are you bald, or is that a wide part?!"

And if anyone said anything to him that he thought

was dumb, he always unleashed his trademark expression, "What are you, a hockey puck?"

Shortly after my wife, Fran, and I married, we were in Las Vegas and I saw that Rickles was performing. I thought Fran would be thrilled to see his show, but when I mentioned it, she recoiled. "Why would I want to waste my time watching such a nasty, mean man?"

I had met Don many times. He belonged to the same country club, Hillcrest, that my father belonged to. On many Sunday brunches at the club, Rickles and his family had sat at a nearby table and had interacted with the Murray clan. He was a frequent guest at Dad's home and my sister Diane liked him so much, she invited Don to her wedding. In all those interactions, he was warm, friendly and loving. So when Fran said she didn't want to see his show because he was a horrible person, I had to drag her, kicking and screaming, to see him perform.

This was a dinner show and we were at ringside. As luck would have it, I had talked with Don at length at the country club a few days earlier, so when he looked down from the stage and saw me, he recognized me. "Look who's here – Jan Murray's son. What's your name again?" "Warren!" I called back. He responded, "I'm sorry?" I responded, louder, "WARREN!" He said, "I heard you – I'm just sorry!" "You know," he continued, "you look just like your father – old and wrinkled!"

And then he went off to attack others in the audience.

When the show ended, he received a standing ovation. A moment later, waiters arrived at each table where Rickles had attacked someone – and presented the victims a bottle of champagne! Included with each bottle was a signed note from him thanking his subjects for being such good sports.

I took Fran backstage to his dressing room and Don greeted us with open arms. He gave Fran a big hug, treated us to share his huge platter of cheese, veggies, dips, cold cuts, crackers, and drinks. We chatted for close to an hour and when we left, Fran turned to me and exclaimed, "What a nice man!"

Fran and me with Don Rickles

Don left us recently and to his public he will always be remembered as an insult comic. But to those of us who were lucky enough to know the real Don Rickles, we will always treasure him as a brilliant comedian and an exceptional human being.

"SANFORD AND SON"

"Sanford and Son," starring comedian Redd Foxx, aired from 1972 to 1977 and was, for that time, the highest rated NBC sitcom in that network's history. Foxx, the star of the series, was a BLACK man named REDD who specialized in "BLUE" material.

At the height of the show's popularity, Foxx got into a salary dispute with the producers. He felt that as the star of the number one comedy on TV, he should be paid more. When he was turned down, he walked off the show for several episodes.

That meant that DeMond Wilson, who played Fred Sanford's son, Lamont, in the series, would have to carry the show in Foxx's absence. With that added responsibility, he, too, demanded a raise to what Foxx was making and he also wanted equal billing. The producers said they'd talked it over and invited Wilson to their office for their decision. As Wilson got off the elevator, he walked by two dozen young, male Black actors, reading "Sanford and Son" scripts, there to audition for the role of Redd Foxx's son! By the time Wilson reached the producer's door, he no longer wanted a raise – he just wanted to keep his job!

Foxx returned to the series the following season and stayed with the show until it folded. I got to know him well in the midst of the show's run, when I headed NBC's Comedy Programming department. I frequently peeked into his dressing room to say hello and see if Redd needed anything. Each and every time I entered his dressing room, the top of the large coffee table in front of his sofa was filled with numerous lines of cocaine! Redd would invariably invite me to try some, but I would always decline. "C'mon, have some coke," he'd offer. "No, thanks, Redd," I'd reply, "I'm trying to lose weight. Do you have any DIET coke?" And Redd would laugh and observe, "You're funnier than your old man."

My favorite character on the show was Fred Sanford's "ugly" aunt, Esther, played by the hilarious comedienne, LaWanda Page. In real life, LaWanda and Redd were lifelong friends, having grown up together in St. Louis. Starting off her career as a fire-eater in small clubs, LaWanda transitioned to standup. If you thought Redd Foxx had a raunchy, off-color act, you should have heard Page's routines! It was not surprising that when Foxx was cast as Fred Sanford, he lobbied for Page to play his aunt Esther. The producers resisted, saying she had no television experience, but Redd threatened to walk if LaWanda wasn't hired. She got the role and was marvelous for all 136 episodes of "Sanford."

I was a big fan of hers, so when I got my job at NBC, I made it my business to show up at all the tapings of Sanford and Son, mostly so I could meet LaWanda. The first time I saw her, she was sitting backstage during a run-through of that week's episode. Wearing my executive power suit, I ambled over to her and, filled with self-importance and wanting to impress her, I introduced myself. "Miss Page," I announced, "I'm Warren Murray. I head the Comedy Programming department at NBC." She looked me over and sweetly commanded, "Be a dear and get me a cup of coffee!"

Properly put in my place, I inquired, "How would you like it?"

"Black like me and sweet like you!" she teased.

That was the start of a beautiful friendship. A few months later, I saw her again backstage, sitting in almost total darkness, running her lines in her head. I almost didn't see her because LaWanda, a very dark-skinned woman, was wearing a black turban, a black turtleneck shirt, black pants, black socks and black shoes. She spotted me and smiled. "What do you think of my new look?" she asked.

Without thinking, I immediately answered, "LaWanda, you look like a mudslide!"

I instantly tried to grab those words and shove them back in my mouth, but the toothpaste, as they say, was already out of the tube. I imagined Page lodging a formal complaint with my bosses at NBC and losing my job. Instead, Page let out a loud shriek of laughter! For the next several minutes, she stopped everyone she saw and repeated my mudslide line, roaring with laughter each time she delivered the punch line.

I left NBC a year before Sanford finished its run, and even wrote an episode for the show that was well received by the producers and cast. But I never got a laugh for any line I wrote like the one I ad-libbed to LaWanda Page.

SUBWAYS

None of the five boroughs of New York were built for cars. Streets were laid out for horse-drawn vehicles, with apartments, stores, skyscrapers, schools and houses of worship sprouting up like crabgrass on both sides of the narrow roads.

By the 1950s, cars, buses, trucks, taxis, bikes and motorcycles jockeyed for position on every street. Drivers honked, cursed, cut each other off and ignored traffic signals in a constant battle to inch forward. Road rage was the norm, not the exception. The only hand signal was made with one finger.

This is why for most of us who grew up in New York, the main form of transportation was the subway.

Growing up in Brooklyn, subways became the means by which I connected with the outside world. Because just about everyone used them, all the seats were usually occupied by the time I got on. I often had to stand, sometimes for my entire trip.

There were two ways to stand in a subway car. There were straps hanging down over all the seats. You could hold on to one of those straps with one hand while you read a newspaper or book with the other. Since there were seated passengers under each strap, whenever the car lurched or went around a curve, you'd bang into someone's knees. On a long ride, say from Brooklyn to midtown Manhattan, you and the seated passenger could easily arrive black and blue.

The other way of standing was holding on to the floor-to-ceiling poles located throughout the cars. During rush hour, as many as five people wrapped their hands around the pole at the same time. Our faces were inches from each other, and if one of them had really bad breath, there was no place to hide.

In October of 1959 I was riding the subway to Brooklyn from the Heights Campus of NYU, where I was taking a full load of classes during my freshman year. I had finished my last class of the day and, although I lived in the dorms on campus, I was headed to Brooklyn for some of my mom's home cooking. The subway was jammed with rush hour passengers, so I found an empty space on a pole and grabbed it. There were four others sharing the pole and our faces were inches apart. Subway cars were not air conditioned and the combination of body odor and halitosis was overpowering. The car was so full, our bodies were pressed together like sardines. If I had let go of the pole, there was no way I could fall.

I had brought a copy of "Dante's Inferno" with me, which I had to read over the weekend for a literature class I was taking. It was unlike anything I had ever read when I attended Erasmus Hall High School. Erasmus, like all public schools in New York, routinely banned any book that contained profanity. Did they really believe that high school students had never heard or used those banned words? Nevertheless, it was still a jolt to my 17-year-old sensibilities when I read, "And there, among the felons in that pit were some who might or might not have been tonsured –

one could not tell, they were so smeared with SHIT!" This so shocked my senses, I burst out laughing – right into the faces of the four people I was tethered to!

Startled, they tried to turn their heads and evade my torrent of laughter. But, they couldn't move. So, one by one, they, too began to laugh. Soon, everyone in the car was shrieking hysterically!

Just as the volume of laughter reached a crescendo, the subway pulled into a station and the doors opened. The people who had been waiting for the train on the platform started to surge forward when they were confronted by a mighty chorus of unrestrained laughter. The new would-be passengers stopped in their tracks, took in the sight and sounds of a car full of clearly deranged individuals, and backed out, fearfully, onto the platform!

The door closed. No one had entered our car. This set off a new round of even more raucous, insane laughter, which lasted all the way to my stop in Brooklyn!

As you can see, privacy was non-existent in subways. Most cars, especially the older ones that I recall, had two long rows of bench seats facing each other. I think that's why most New Yorkers always took something to read with them when they rode. If you didn't, you had to stare straight ahead, usually at the person sitting directly in front of you.

I hated when people across from me stared straight ahead. Even if they were lost in thought and clearly not paying attention to me, I always felt they were gazing at me like birds of prey.

After a while, I developed a defense strategy. I would stare back at that person, then slowly lower my eyes until I was seemingly studying their crotch! Then I would break out into a grin and maybe even a low giggle. The passenger would usually become very self-conscious, wondering if their fly was open, or if there was some hideous stain there! The next time we reached a station, they would usually bolt out the door, dying from embarrassment!

One time I was lucky enough to find a seat in a packed subway car. A young woman grabbed the strap above my head and held on while the train lurched forward. After a while, I noticed she was making faces like she was in pain. I asked, "Are you okay?" She answered, "Not really. I'm a little dizzy because I'm pregnant." I immediately got up and gave her my seat. Now I was holding the strap. The pained expression on her face instantly disappeared. I smiled down at her and observed, "I'm glad you're feeling better, but, pardon me for saying this, you don't really look pregnant." "Well," she confided, "It's only been ten minutes!"

Such were the games New Yorkers played in order to get seats on subways and buses. If that's what made us rude, loud and pushy to the rest of the country, it was simply a rite of passage. Darwin had a term for it: "Survival of the fittest."

Subways were noisy, smelly, dirty Petri dishes, but if you ask, most New Yorkers wouldn't trade them for the bumper-to-bumper highways most Americans have to endure today.

SEX

I was a happy child for my first 14 years. Then I discovered sex. To be honest, it discovered me. Hormones I never knew existed kicked in and for the next 60 years my brain and my schmekel (Yiddish for penis) fought a never-ending battle for control of my mind and my body.

I had my first sexual experience when I was 14. Unfortunately, I was alone at the time! Still, it opened up my eyes to a whole new world of possibilities. Suddenly, girls weren't yucky anymore. I began to spend most of my time mentally undressing every girl I came into contact with. My mom told me I was just going through a phase. I'd outgrow it, she assured me, in about a half a century. I had my first "sex talk" from my mother. Her biggest concern was that I'd get someone pregnant. "Sex is a drive," she counseled, "so don't be a reckless driver."

A friend of mine gave me a condom, which I kept in my wallet "just in case." I carried it in my wallet for so long, it made a permanent circular dent in the leather. I wasn't real popular with the opposite sex. One time a girl phoned me and said, "Come on over, there's nobody home." I went over. There was nobody home!

The girl who became my "first" had a spectacular figure and a reputation to match. She was so sexy, the birds and bees studied HER!

I was lucky to have been sexually active during the sexual revolution. With the advent of "the pill," women began to explore their sexuality with gusto. I remember meeting a lovely lass at a party. We both agreed to indulge in a "one night stand." When we finished our lovemaking, I realized that I really liked her. I confided to her, "I'd really like to see more of you." She looked at me with a puzzled expression and said, "There's nothing more of me to see!"

I gradually discovered that the two most important things in life were sex and laughter. Unfortunately, I used to achieve them both at the same time!

Everyone was smoking in the 60s and it was true that lighting up after coitus was a real thing. I remember asking my date, after a strenuous session, "Do you smoke after sex?" She answered, "Gee, I never looked!"

When you're young, you tend to experiment with all kinds of positions and different forms of sex. I remember one girl telling me that she was open to almost every form of sex but that she had a real problem with oral sex. I asked her what the problem was. She replied, "For one thing – the view!"

To me, everything was on the table as long as both parties agreed to it. As Alfred Kinsey once proclaimed, "The only unnatural sex act is the one you can't perform."

For a short time I roomed with a black student at

NYU named Fred Clark. He was a basketball player on the freshman squad. He had powerful muscles and a flat, ribbed stomach. We shared a small room in the dorm, and we often saw each other in the buff. One day he spotted me coming out of the shower and asked, "Hey, roommate, what's twelve inches long and white?" Before I could answer, he shouted, "Nothing!"

I've discovered that as we get older, the things we took for granted our body could do – we can't do anymore. First, things start to slow down, then they stop and start and stop again. You begin to worry and eventually to panic. "Worry" is the first time you can't do it a second time. "Panic" is the second time you can't do it the first time!

At 79, I feel like I'm still part of the sexual revolution, only now I'm out of ammunition.

Nowadays, a "quickie before dinner" is a nap!

A "three-way" is a bulb!

If it weren't for pickpockets, I'd have no sex life at all!

Don't get me wrong, at my age I still "satisfy" my wife every night. For example, last night Fran and I were in bed. I looked over to her and gave her my sexiest look and whispered, "Honey – I'm too tired to do anything." And she smiled back and replied, "I'm satisfied!"

Just kidding. Even in our late 70s, Fran and I make love almost every night of the week: Almost Monday... almost Tuesday...!

Since my four grandsons might read this book, here are some things I've learned about sex that I think they should know:

Casual sex is fine – you don't have to wear a tie!

Condoms should be used on every conceivable occasion!

Kids in a car's back seat cause accidents – accidents in the car's back seat cause kids!

Never have sex with a female clown – she'll twist your penis into a poodle!

After sex, never ask your partner, "Was it good for you?" I did that once and she answered, "I don't think it was good for anybody!"

Also never ask, "On a scale from one to ten, how did I do tonight?" She just might respond, "You know I'm not good with fractions!"

Never have sex with your teacher – especially if you're home-schooled!

And my final thought on the subject is this – there are things better than sex and things worse than sex – but you'll never find anything quite like it.

BARBRA STREISAND

Barbra Streisand is one of the greatest performers of our time. She has won every major award in show business -- Oscars, Emmys, Tonys, Grammys, Golden Globes, Best in Show – everything!

But when I knew her, she was my classmate at Erasmus Hall High School in Brooklyn. We both graduated in the class of 1959. Under her yearbook picture, it said "Choral Club" and "Chorus."

STREISAND, BARBARA
Freshman Chorus, 1, 2; Choral Club, 2-4.

Actually, I didn't know her. I never even knew she attended Erasmus until years after we graduated. I discovered we were classmates from my father. He told the following two stories about Streisand a bazillion times, so I believe they happened.

When I was a senior at NYU, Dad called me at my fraternity house and said he had attended a Broadway show, "I Can Get It For You Wholesale," and saw a young performer who he believed was going to be a superstar. Her name was Barbra Streisand, a name that meant nothing to me at that time. Dad went on to say that he went backstage after the show to her dressing room and introduced himself to her. He said, "Hi, Barbra, I'm Jan Murray." To which she replied, "Hi, Jan. How's Warren?" My father was stunned. "How do you know my son?" And she responded with this story:

In my senior year, she learned that my father was a headliner in Las Vegas. She concocted a plan to make me notice her in the hopes that I would ask her out, date her, and eventually take her home to meet the famous Jan Murray. Somehow, she'd figure out a way to sing for him and he'd be so enthralled by her voice that he'd make her his opening act in Vegas! And that's how she'd jump-start her career in show business!

Obviously that never happened. In my senior year I was going steady with a wonderful girl named Gaile, so if Barbra was trying to catch my eye, I simply didn't notice. Years later, when Dad and I reminisced about Streisand, he berated me thusly: "If you had paid attention to her, you putz, YOU could have been her first ex-husband!"

About a decade later, Dad's close friend, Buddy Hackett, took him to a celebrity charity art auction. Dad wasn't a collector and didn't want to go, but Buddy insisted that he'd get a kick out of it. Attending the auction would be comedians, singers, actors, producers, etc. So Dad went and was so bored he was about to leave when the auctioneer introduced a painting that he loved and wanted to have.

The bidding started at $500 but he figured he'd put a quick end to the bidding by shouting, "One thousand!"

Ten rows in front of him sat a woman, dressed in black with a veil covering her face. She looked like a Mafia widow from "The Godfather." She chirped, "A thousand and ONE!"

My father was stunned. He was being outbid by a dollar?! He countered with, "TWO thousand!" The woman immediately bellowed, "And ONE!"

Dad was now a wild man. He was going to own that painting, even if he had to re-mortgage his Beverly Hills home. He kept upping his bid and the woman kept adding one dollar to his bid until, finally, he prevailed. For a painting he thought he'd buy for a thousand bucks, he wound up paying $6,000!

When the auction ended, Dad stood in line to give his payment information and collect his painting. Hackett approached him and insisted that Dad leave the line to meet his good friend. Dad agreed and Buddy walked him over to – the veiled woman who had driven up his bid!

"This is your good friend?!" Dad hissed, angrily. Before Buddy could answer, the woman lifted her veil, revealing Barbra Streisand! Her first words were, "Hi, Jan, how's Warren?"

My father only met Barbra Streisand twice in his whole life, and both times her first words to him were, "How's Warren?"

My postscript to these stories is that although I had a long and fairly successful career in show business as a writer, producer and network executive, I never did meet Ms. Streisand. So if you're reading this, Barbra – I'm fine!

TEACHING

With a master's degree from Columbia University, I embarked on a teaching career in September of 1964. I was married to my first wife and we had a one-bedroom apartment in Spring Valley, New York, a suburb about an hour's drive from NYC.

The school was called Kakiat Junior High School. (They didn't have middle schools back then.) I was to teach eighth grade American History and be paid $5,000 a year! The plan was for me to teach there until I retired. Once I received tenure, I couldn't be fired unless I mooned the class, so teaching, despite its poor compensation, did provide lifetime job security. And after twelve years of teaching, I would reach the top of the pay scale, which in 1964 was a whopping $14,000! With that much money, we could buy a house and a new car!

I couldn't wait to start teaching and, in the words of Lee Iacocca, "pass civilization on to a new generation."

My first day at school got off to a bizarre start. As I walked towards the front doors of the school, I noticed a circle of young students staring at something. They were cheering, "Go! Go! Go! You can do it!" I worked my way through the crowd and saw two dogs, one large and one small. The small one was trying to mount the larger dog! I tried to disperse the crowd and separate the dogs. I failed at both efforts. Finally, the Principal of the school, Ray Chissamore, came out. He blew a whistle and shouted into a bullhorn that any student who was late for his first class would be given detention. The students reluctantly left the dogs and entered the school. If this were today, the dogs would have gone viral on social media. Dr. Chissamore smiled at me. "How do you like teaching so far?" he asked me with a wink.

My first class entered. They seemed excited, bright and eager to learn. I discovered later that the first week or two of school is referred to as "the honeymoon" by teachers. By that, they mean that the students appear to be hanging on your every word and worshipping the wise mentor before them. In reality, they are sizing up the teacher, carefully looking for any weaknesses they can exploit for their benefit. "What can I get away with in Mr. Murray's class?" is what they're thinking. Starting in week three, they begin testing the teacher, to see how much they can get away with before they're reprimanded.

I knew nothing of this on Day One. After the Pledge of Allegiance and morning announcements concluded over the loudspeaker, I addressed my first class. "Good morning, everyone, I'm Mr. Murray and this is wood shop." Immediately, there was a chorus of gasps. Kids began looking at their programs frantically. I laughed. "Just kidding. This is American History." Some laughed, some sighed with relief and others gave me dirty looks.

"In a couple of days," I intoned, "I'll make a seating chart so I can get to know you faster. But for today, I will just read off your names in alphabetical order. If you're here, raise your hand and say 'HERE.' If you're absent, raise your hand and say 'ABSENT.'"

Not only didn't anyone laugh, but most of the hands in the class were thrust up in the air. I picked a boy and he asked, "How can I raise my hand and say ABSENT if I'm absent?" My immediate thought was "tough room." I made it clear to them that once again, I was joking. This was met with mostly puzzled expressions on their orthodontic faces.

I decided to move on. "Your grade will be based on your test scores, your class participation and whether or not you laugh at my jokes!" The class quickly erupted into loud, fake laughter. "That wasn't a joke!" I shouted. The class instantly fell silent. I smiled at them. "Actually, it was." The class panicked. Should they laugh or not?

I was told later that what I had done was a good thing. I had kept them off-balance. They left the room still wondering what weaknesses I possessed that they could exploit. I'd like to note here that of all the education courses I took at Columbia, not a single professor ever mentioned the importance of keeping my class off-balance.

Even though this was American history, I always began each day's lesson with current events. I would pick two students to read the newspaper and report on one of the stories they read. It couldn't be about sports, comics, horoscopes or advice to the lovelorn. They were to choose something from the first section that was of national, international or local interest. At first, they groaned, but when I announced I would give "extra credit" for each report, everyone's hand was raised. One boy asked why we were doing current events in a history class. I reminded him that "today's current event is tomorrow's history." He shrugged and muttered "whatever," so I took that for acceptance of my explanation.

It has been over four decades since that first day I stood before a class, but I still remember the first current events report I heard. A girl named Nadine talked about China revisiting its "one child per family" government policy. So many couples had protested the policy that Peking (it wasn't called Beijing yet) was seriously considering allowing couples to have two children instead of one.

I thanked her for her report and used it to launch into a discussion of the effects of overpopulation on the world's food supply. I showed them how, according to Thomas Malthus, the world's food supply grew arithmetically, from 1 to 2 to 3 to 4, while population grew geometrically, from 1 to 2 to 4 to 8. Eventually, there would be too many people, not enough food, and this could result in mass starvation, wars, and maybe even the end of the world! I added that China already had over a billion people, so doubling births could be a disaster in the near future. "After all," I warned, "One out of every six children in the world is already Chinese."

The girl who gave the report raised her hand and I called on her.

"Is this going to be on a test?" she asked.

I told her "no."

"Then why do we have to know this,?" she demanded.

I looked at her thoughtfully. "How old are you, Nadine?" I asked.

"Fourteen."

"Ah," I responded. "That means you might be married four years from now."

"So?"

"So," I concluded, "if you have six children, your sixth child will be Chinese!"

I admit I fully expected the class to roar with laughter. Instead, they stared at me, puzzled. Nadine's eyes and mouth opened wide in horror.

The next day I was called into the Principal's office.

Dr. Chissamore didn't seem pleased. "Did you tell Nadine Von Lowenstein that she was going to have a Chinese baby?" he snarled. I gulped and related everything that led up to my joke. He leaned back in his chair and explained to me that 14-year-olds don't have developed senses of humor. "They laugh at fart jokes, bodily noises, and people slipping on banana peels. Anything clever is lost on them and results in me getting angry phone calls from parents." I assured him I understood. "The next time I get the urge to make them laugh," I assured him, "I'll keep my mouth shut and just ask them to pull my finger!"

For a while, I stifled my constant urge to inject humor into my daily lessons. Then, one day, I was discussing Sir Francis Drake in class. Drake had been commissioned by Queen Elizabeth to attack Spanish galleons that were returning to Spain with millions in gold. His men were called "Sea Dogs" although, truth be told, they were simply British pirates.

Whenever Drake went into battle, he always asked for his red coat. When his First Mate approached to say that a Spanish treasure ship had been spotted, Drake would roar, "Fetch me my red coat!" The officer saluted, but before he went to get the coat he asked Drake, "If you don't mind me asking, Captain, why do you always ask for your red coat before you go into battle?"

Drake replied, "The coat is the same color as blood. If I'm wounded, I don't want my men to see me bleeding and lose heart."

"Brilliant!" the First Mate declared, as he dashed off to get Drake his red coat.

"A week or so later," I continued to the class, "The First Mate reappeared and announced that he had spotted a Spanish warship off the port side."

"Fetch me my red coat!" Drake thundered.

"There are also warships off the starboard, bow and stern! Captain, we are completely surrounded!"

"In that case," Drake commanded, "fetch me my brown pants!"

There was a moment of stunned silence in the classroom. The students wondered if they had heard right. Had Mr. Murray actually told a shit joke? Finally, they couldn't contain themselves. They shrieked with laughter that could be heard throughout the school.

I had found their level. And more importantly, they never forgot Sir Francis Drake.

Years later, when I was living in California and working at the studios, a student from my first teaching year at Kakiat spotted me while I was in a CVS parking lot. He introduced himself and told me I had been his favorite teacher growing up. I thanked him for the compliment. Suddenly, he looked at me strangely and asked, "Hey, Mr. Murray, are you expecting someone to attack you?" I answered, "No. Why would you ask me that?" And he replied, "Because you're wearing your brown pants!"

On the day I received my notice of tenure at Kakiat, I resigned. I was determined to move to California and give comedy writing a try while I was still young. It wasn't until more than two decades of writing and two wives later that I found myself in front of a classroom again.

The name of the school was Los Cerritos Middle School, located in Thousand Oaks, California. My starting salary was $42,000, a lot more than I received at Kakiat JHS, but a lot less than I made from writing and producing. It's true that people don't go into teaching for the money. You have to genuinely love working with kids and have a passion for the subject you're teaching.

I taught at Los Cerritos for 14 years and loved most of it. I always made sure I injected my particular brand of humor into every lesson I constructed. I tried to depict myself as a sort of Robin Williams-esque presence in the classroom. Most of the kids seemed to embrace my frenetic approach to teaching. They erected a sign that graced my classroom door. It read "Room one – where History is fun!"

To better understand the Constitution and how the system of checks and balances is supposed to work, I had my classes create their own island countries. They had to write their own constitutions and describe how the concept of democracy would work and be safeguarded in their nations. If their constitution differed from America's, they had to explain why they had made changes to our "perfect" constitution. To 13- and 14-year-olds, this sounded like a tedious bore-fest, so I had to figure out what the funny side was to creating a constitution. So, to make it fun, I had them also create their own flag, national anthem, and demonstrate some customs that were unique to their country, like a national dance or handshake. During the presentations of their respective countries, the students not only explained how their government would be run, they also sang, danced and choreographed complicated and hilarious handshakes that sometimes took several minutes to execute.

American novelist Gail Godwin once said, "Great teaching is one-quarter preparation and three-quarters theater." I agree. I prepared lessons like they were the final draft of a comedy show episode. The lesson worked even better if the students, themselves, had parts in the episode.

One day I asked all the students in the front desk of each row to rise, take all their books, and stand in the back of the room in one corner. I then ordered the rest of the class to move forward one desk. The kids I had moved to the rear protested loudly, some angrily, some whining, "Hey, that's my seat!" "I can't see from the back of the room!" "How long do I have to stand here?"

"For the rest of the semester," I informed them, mock-sternly.

"No fair!" they groaned. "We didn't do anything." "It's uncomfortable standing here, holding our books for 45 minutes!"

I ignored them and addressed the seated students. "Today," I began, "we will study how the American government kicked the Native Americans off their land and forced them to live on very inhospitable and uncomfortable reservations!"

For a moment there was silence. Then, one by one, as the light bulbs suddenly lit over each of their heads, they began to clap and cheer. It was a scene out of dozens of Hollywood movies. The "slow clap" was actually happening in my class!

I've always felt that if you simply lecture students, their eyes glaze over and they lose interest. But if you can somehow get them mentally and physically involved in the material, they'll stay focused and maybe even learn something.

Through the years certain students have stood out in my memory. I had a boy who only raised his hand when he wanted a bathroom pass. There was a girl who said "like" after every word. She once gave a report on George Washington. "He was like our first like President. He like served like two terms like in office!" When she finished, she asked me how she did on her report. I answered, "I like LIKED it!" She was like not amused.

It's not considered educationally correct to scold a pupil for doing sub-par work these days. I told one boy he wasn't trying and might fail if he didn't get his act together. He growled back, "You're destroying my shellfish steam!"

I noticed that through the years, most students have grown lazy when it comes to schoolwork. Only a small percentage of them strive to get As. Most seem okay with maintaining a nautical average – below C level! I'm convinced a teenager's mind starts working the moment he wakes up – and doesn't stop until he gets to class!

And they cheat a lot more than they did when I first started teaching in New York. My students tried everything, except studying. Two girls would drop their test papers on the ground between their desks and pick up their friend's paper. After making whatever changes they deemed necessary, they dropped them again and returned them to the original test taker.

Others weren't so subtle. They wrote information, in ink, on their wrists and on the inside of their palms. Others taped notes on the backs of the students in front of them. Some even learned Morse Code so they could tap out answers with their pencils. Sometimes the room sounded like a Woodpecker convention!

When I was teaching English, I assigned the class to read a novel. One boy turned in a report on "Cheaper By the Dozen." He wrote, "This is a heartwarming story about a couple who have 12 children. The main characters in the book are Steve Martin and Bonnie Hunt!"

When I was writing and producing comedies, I followed a tradition of putting together a "Blooper Reel" of outtakes that occurred during the shooting season. These usually consisted of flubbed lines, props that didn't work, doors that wouldn't open, etc. They were played before the cast and crew at the annual Christmas party and everyone would shriek with laughter at all the mistakes that were made that the public never got to see. I carried on that tradition as a teacher.

Through my 14 years at Los Cerritos Middle School, I often had to grade essays. Whenever I came upon a "blooper," I wrote it down and stuck it in my folder, mainly to amuse myself when the strains of teaching bore down on me. What follows are actual sentences that my students wrote on essays over a 14-year span:

"People in America have a right to show their stomachs and their skin."

"Your country is where you live, and if you don't live where you live, why are you living there?"

"America is different from other planets."

"The Ford was invented by Harrison Ford."

"Americans have a 75% chance of not getting killed."

"In other countries, people take their friends for granite."

"I have visited many other countries, like my grandma's house."

"We won our freedom from the British and became our own country. Then we became a continent."

"American scientists work 24/7 on different cures for cancer, oldtimer's disease, and how to use the thing we have to use as an alternative organ."

"When Marco Polo discovered America, blacks and whites moved there to be free. The slaves were freed by Martin Luther King."

"In third world countries, entertainment is singing, dancing and intercourse. Many Americans take these pleasures for granted. I appreciate these fun activities."

"America has a lot of nature, so we won't run out of air."

"In America, women are thought of as normal individuals."

"America is not only a country, it's a place where people live."

"Good weather makes us good citizens."

"The kids of today are the people of tomorrow."

"In America, our rights are guaranteed by the first ten commandments."

"America's most important law is the seat-belt law."

"Our flag represents all of our 52 states."

"My parents moved to America in 1970-ish."

"I'm out of ideas, so 'bye.'"

There you have it. And you wonder where the next generation of politicians is coming from. The famed comedian, Art Linkletter, once said, "Kids say the darndest things." As you can see, he was right.

I never won an Emmy as a writer, but I did win a prestigious award as a teacher. It was 2001 and I had only been back in the classroom for seven years. I was in the middle of teaching a lesson when the door to my room opened and a man and woman entered. The man carried a hand-held television camera on his shoulder with an NBC logo on it. The woman held a small, portable microphone. "Are you Warren Murray?" she asked.

Startled, I answered in the affirmative.

"Congratulations!" she said. "You've won the Crystal Apple Award!"

I had no idea what that was. The thought occurred to me that this was some kind of practical joke set up by a fellow teacher. I decided to play along to see where this was going. "The WHAT award?" I inquired.

"The Crystal Apple Award," she repeated. "What do you have to say about that?"

"Well," I responded, "At my age, I thought I'd win the

Crystal PRUNE award!"

The reporter faced her cameraman and yelled "CUT!" Then she turned and scolded me.

"Mr. Murray, this is a very prestigious award. Hundreds of teachers were nominated and we interviewed principals, teachers, parents and even students before you were chosen. Please show it the respect it deserves."

Chastised, I promised her I'd be good. She signaled the cameraman to start taping.

"Mr. Murray," she resumed, "you have won the Crystal Apple Award and..."

I cut her off. "Excuse me, but what exactly is this award for?"

She rolled her eyes. "You've been named the Outstanding Teacher in Southern California..."

"Wow! That's really something!"

"For the month of November!" she concluded.

"So let me get this straight," I teased, "in September I was so-so; in October, I stunk up the place; but in November – I was the best?!"

"CUT!" she howled. "What's wrong with you?"

As the class laughed uproariously, I pulled her aside. "Listen, there are lots of educators who have been doing this for decades. They're much better teachers than I am. So I can only assume that I won this award because I use humor as a teaching tool. That's what makes me different. So when you interview me, you've got to show that side of me."

She thought about it. "Okay," she sighed, grudgingly. "Just don't belittle the award."

We started again. "Mr. Murray, you were a successful comedy writer and for several years you headed NBC's comedy programming department. Why would you give all of that up to teach?"

I gave her my most sincere look. "For the big bucks!"

She looked at me the way my first two wives used to.

"Just kidding," I continued, "I left show business to teach for two very important reasons – July and August!"

I thought she was going to cry. My class was now hysterical. Somehow, she plodded on and I tried to interject some thoughtful insights and perspectives between my caustic answers. (When the show aired that night, all my jokes were edited out. Only the thoughtful insights and perspectives were shown, making it a very dry interview.)

She presented me with the award, a crystal apple

from Tiffany's, on a base that bears the inscription "Crystal Apple Award – 2001." The apple sits atop my family room fireplace mantle, occupying the exact spot where my Emmy Award should have gone. To be honest, I truly believe I'm prouder of this award than I ever would have been had I won an Emmy.

I retired from teaching in June, 2009, at the age of 67. The staff gave me a huge retirement party, with lots of food and drink. Many of them got up and roasted me. This was fitting, since I was the one they had called on to roast retirees the whole time I taught at Los Cerritos. I only remember fragments of my remarks that day, so here's how I closed out my teaching career:

"Thank you all for this warm and funny send-off. I consider this tribute more than an honor – it's an imposition! I could be home now watching reruns of "Gilligan's Island!"

"I can honestly say that my 14 years at Los Cerritos has given me something I never had before – poverty!"

"All seriousness aside, there's nothing more rewarding or intellectually stimulating than to come to work each day and face 120 horny teenagers!"

"My students, who I lovingly refer to as my 'flatliners,' all seem to think that DUH is a word!"

"That Taco Bell is the Mexican phone company!"

"That the capital of Oklahoma is 'O'!"

"That the moon is closer to us than Iraq because we can see the moon, but we can't see Iraq!"

"That a cesarean section is a district in Rome!"

"That 'don't' is short for 'donut'"

"That dinosaurs died out because of reptile dysfunction!"

"A girl in one of my classes was wearing a t-shirt that said TGIF. I asked her if she knew what that meant. She said, 'Sure – This Goes In Front!'"

"I asked a male student to spell Mississippi. He said, 'The river or the state?'"

"Sometimes I wonder if any of them can even spell I.Q.!"

"They're almost in high school, and they still don't know Roman Numerals. One boy told me the U.S. fought in World War Eleven!"

"We humans keep looking for signs of intelligent life on other planets. I've spent the last 14 years searching for it in my classroom!"

"I'm kidding, of course. Students – you can't live with them ... (long pause) That's it!"

At that point, I thanked everyone who had mentored me and stood by me my whole time at Los Cerritos, and for their patience, productivity and professionalism. I really don't think I could've had any success at all without their advice and support.

I share my Crystal Apple Award with all of them.

If I were to ask you, dear reader, who won the Best Actor or Actress Oscars last year, or who won the Nobel Prize for Literature or Chemistry, you'd probably have a tough time coming up with an answer. But if I ask you to name for me a teacher who had a dramatic and lasting impact on your life, I'm sure that each and every one of you could immediately name that man or woman from your childhood. That's the power that great teachers have. I'm reminding you of this because lately teachers are being replaced by laptops and Powerpoint presentations in our classrooms.

They can be effective tools, but none of them can motivate you, praise you, help you reach your potential – or find the funny side of your lesson.

Support your local teacher!

And yes – this will be on your test!

VENICE

It was 1999 and my wife, Fran, and I found ourselves in Venice, Italy. We had already been to Rome, Florence and Pisa and were thoroughly enchanted by the beauty and history of this country. We started our exploration of Venice with a sightseeing tour that gave us an overall view of the city. It also pointed us to the sights that we absolutely had to examine during our stay.

Since we'd only been married for five years and neither of us had ever been here before, Fran said, somewhat wistfully, "What a breathtaking place! I hope we can do something really romantic here."

I told her I knew just the thing. I took her to an area where you could rent a gondola and quickly booked one. The proprietor asked if we wanted a singer to accompany us. He pointed to a group of men standing in front of a wall. They were all opera singers, and we could choose the one we wanted. One man stood out. He was extremely heavy and reminded me of Pavarotti. I picked him and the singer asked if he could also bring along his accompanist, a young man who played the concertina. I agreed and Fran was over the moon. We were taking a romantic gondola ride in Venice!

The gondolier took us to the middle of the Grand Canal, right next to the famous Rialto Bridge which appears in just about every painting ever made depicting Venice. The canal was much busier than

I imagined. It was filled with other gondolas, water taxis, and motorboats. As we reached the center of the canal, our opera singer stood and began singing "O Solo Mio," much to Fran's delight. A few bars into his rendition of the classic piece, a speedboat zoomed past us, creating huge waves!

Our gondola began to rock. Before I could yell a warning to the singer to sit down, he lost his balance and fell overboard, into the canal!

Fran screamed to me, "Do something!"

I took out my camera and started snapping pictures of the flailing whale in the water!

Eventually, the gondolier, the accompanist and I managed to pull the singer back into the gondola. That task was exhausting as the man's weight almost tipped us over more than once as we tried to get him back in.

I turned to Fran, who was visibly shaken by the whole ordeal and said, in my sexiest voice, "Is this romantic enough for you?"

Back at the dock, we decided to walk along the Grand Canal and look for a restaurant that served authentic Venetian food. We found many, but this being summer, all of them were jammed with tourists and had hours-long wait times. We kept walking and finally came upon a restaurant with outdoor seating overlooking the canal – and we could be seated immediately! Thrilled, we took our seats and were handed our menus. The food items were in Chinese! So on our romantic visit of Venice, we ate moo shu pork and char siu ding, with noodles and rice!

After dinner, we decided to walk to the Rialto Bridge and shop at its stalls. To get there, we had to cross over the Bridge of Sighs. It's called that because it's right next to a prison. As felons crossed over that bridge on the way to incarceration, they often stopped, took a last look at Venice and freedom – and sighed. As we stood on that bridge, a speedboat zoomed underneath us. It was filled with what I can only assume were inebriated college boys. As they came into our sight, they all dropped their pants and mooned us!

You just can't get more romantic than that!

WISHES

We've all read stories since we were young about Genie's granting people wishes. All of us have dreamt about what it would be like to have a wish granted. We wish upon a star and make a wish before we blow out a birthday candle. We never tell anyone what our wish is, because then it won't come true. Every time we ask God for something in our nightly prayers, we're making a wish.

If somehow we could have a single wish granted, would we use that wish for the good of mankind, or for ourselves? Should we end war or win the lottery? Eliminate starvation or become irresistible to the opposite sex?

One of the basic plot devices Rod Serling used in "The Twilight Zone" was someone having his or her wish granted – only to find that what they wished for leads to disaster and unhappiness. One guy wished to become the richest man on Earth, and spent the rest of his life fighting off tax men, women, friends, strangers and relatives – who all wanted him for his money.

A man wishes he could live forever – and gets sentenced to life Imprisonment!

There were dozens of other stories like that, but you get the idea. As a wise man once said, "Be careful what you wish for."

Luckily, comedians have always seen the funny side of wish-granting. Here are a few of my personal favorites:

Phil Foster told me this one:

A guy brings his date to a swap meet and they are approached by a grizzled old man. He tells the couple, "If you buy this mirror and hang it on a door, it will grant each beholder one wish." The guy buys the mirror, brings it home, and hangs it on the door. He and his date flip a coin and the girl wins. She looks in the mirror first and says, "Mirror, mirror on the door, make my boobies 44!"

There's a crash of thunder, a bolt of lightning, and instantly, out spring two magnificent breasts, a perfect set of 44s!

The guy immediately runs in front of the mirror and wishes for the one thing he wants most in the world. He says, "Mirror, mirror on the door, make my pecker touch the floor!"

There is a crack of thunder, a bolt of lightning, and instantly – his legs begin to get shorter and shorter!

My favorite wish-fulfillment story also involved a mirror. It was my father's favorite story and he told it onstage countless times:

A little eight-year-old boy comes home from school and on the way to his room, he passes his teenage sister's door. He hears loud moaning coming from her room. He opens the door a crack a peeks in. He sees his sister standing in front of a full-length mirror, stark naked! She's running her hands up and down the front of her body and moans, "I wish I had a man! I wish I had a man!"

The little boy gets all embarrassed and rushes to his room. The next day, he comes home from school and once more passes his sister's room. This time, he hears nothing. Curious, he opens the door a crack and peers in. He sees his sister in bed – with a man!

The little boy immediately rushes to his room, takes off all his clothes, stands in front of a full-length mirror, runs his hands up and down his body, and moans, "I wish I had a bicycle! I wish I had a bicycle!"

There are scores of "wish" jokes, usually involving a genie and three wishes, but they all have the same format. A person makes a wish, it comes true, and it comically screws up his life!

If I had a free wish, I'd wish for a trillion more wishes. Since it appears that wishes have about the same odds of coming true as the odds are of winning the Mega Millions or the Publisher's Clearing House sweepstakes, I'd gladly settle for cashing in on just one. Maybe I'd be 6' 4", or speak French fluently, or play ragtime piano like Scott Joplin, or live in a world free from pandemics, or be able to eat all the chocolate I want without gaining weight, or – my personal number one wish – sell a million copies of *FUNNY SIDE UP*!

HENNY YOUNGMAN

Before Steven Wright, the undisputed "King of One-liners" was Henny Youngman. Whereas most comedians in the 50s, 60s and 70s had fully developed routines that were delivered in 15 to 20- minute "chunks," Youngman peppered his audiences with a machine-gun barrage of totally unrelated jokes:

"A man goes to a psychiatrist and the shrink asks him what he does for a living. The man says, 'I'm an auto mechanic.' The psychiatrist says, 'Get UNDER the couch!'"

"Speaking of horses ..." (Note: No one was speaking of horses) "I bet on a horse that was so slow, the jockey kept a diary of the trip!"

"Take my wife – please!"

That was his trademark saying. His wife, Sadie, constantly bore the brunt of Henny's endless supply of "wife jokes."

"Can my wife talk. We were in Miami Beach and when we got home, her tongue was sunburned!"

"My wife doesn't take weight off – she just rearranges it!"

"Want to drive your wife crazy? Don't talk in your sleep – just grin!"

"Last night I surprised my wife by ordering both our meals in French. It was a Chinese restaurant!"

"I took my wife to the Great Wall of China. She wouldn't talk to me for a week. She thought we were going to the Great MALL of China!"

"My wife snores, so I bought ear plugs. After she falls asleep, I stick them in her nose!"

"I haven't spoken to my wife in two years – I don't like to interrupt her!"

"My wife wanted me to buy her something that went from zero to 200 in under five seconds – so I bought her a scale!"

I knew Henny well. He and Sadie lived in Brooklyn for many years, right near the apartment I lived in with my mother and grandmother. (I saw my father on weekends and holidays after the divorce.) His son, Gary, and I were friends and I once spent a weekend in Youngman's summer retreat in Woodstock, New York. (Yes, THAT Woodstock.)

Once, when I was dating a girl in Chicago, I took her to see Henny who was performing at Mr. Kelly's, a famous nightclub in the Windy City. I was told the show was sold out. Disappointed, I wrote a note to Henny, telling him I was there and was sorry I couldn't get in to see the show. I tipped the maître d' and he delivered the note backstage. While my date and I were in front of the club, waiting for our car, the maître d' rushed out and told us to come back inside. We saw several men carrying a table to the front of the stage. It was quickly set up and the maître d' escorted us to our seats. "Mr. Youngman said to tell you he's thrilled you're here. Dinner's on him and he wants you to go backstage after the show."

That's the kind of man he was. When we went backstage, Youngman told us a story about his early days in show business that I'd like to share with you:

When Youngman was a young man, his agent called and told him he'd gotten him a small role in a movie. He was to fly to California for a one-week shoot.

Henny was ecstatic, not so much about being in a film, but because he'd heard so many stories about "wild Hollywood parties." He begged his agent to get him invited to one of those legendary orgies. The agent wasn't thrilled about this. He felt that "pimp" wasn't part of his job description. But Henny was a rising star and he wanted to keep his client happy, so he reluctantly said he'd try.

When Youngman arrived at his hotel in Hollywood, he got a call from his agent. He had gotten Henny invited to Clark Gable's home in Beverly Hills for the wild party the young comic had asked to attend.

In addition to Gable, Jimmy Stewart, Spencer Tracy, Bert Lancaster and Kirk Douglas would be there. Youngman could care less. "What about the women?" the young, single, horny comic shrieked. "What women stars will be there?"

The agent rattled off a "Who's Who" of female stars. "Rita Hayworth, Barbara Stanwyck, Claudette Colbert and Katherine Hepburn will be there!"

Henny was thrilled. He'd actually be a participant in a legendary wild Hollywood party. He drove to Gable's mansion and was greeted by a butler with a thick British accent. Entering the spacious entry foyer, Youngman noticed two piles of clothes stacked up next to the imposing spiral staircase. One contained men's clothing, coats, slacks, shirts, ties, socks and underwear. The other pile had women's garments, including bras and panties!

The butler informed Henny that all the guests were in the dining room – au natural! Youngman couldn't believe his luck. He was going to see the most beautiful and famous women in Hollywood in the nude! He immediately disrobed and tossed his clothes on top of the men's pile. The butler instructed him to swing open the French doors and join the others. They were expecting him.

Henny flung open the doors, his arms spread-eagled, and announced, stark naked, "Have no fear, Youngman's here!"

Seated at the table were all of the aforementioned film stars – dressed to the hilt in formal attire!

As Henny looked on in horror and humiliation, someone tapped him on his shoulder. He turned and standing behind him was his agent.

"You asked me to get you into a wild Hollywood party, Henny. This is pretty wild, huh?"

Before he could choke his agent to death, all the stars, who were willing participants in this elaborate practical joke, burst out laughing, rose, and gave Henny a standing ovation! They also invited him to join them for dinner, after he put his clothes back on, of course.

Henny never did attend a wild Hollywood party, but he got something better – a great story to tell.

The last time I saw Youngman was in the late 1980s. I read that he was appearing in a comedy club on Ventura Boulevard in Encino, California. I bought a ticket and watched the show. Henny looked much older than I remembered and was at the tail end of his fabulous 70-plus-year career.

His audience consisted of fans who had aged with him and had come to pay homage to a comedy legend. Henny didn't disappoint. For over an hour, Youngman delighted the crowd with a torrent of vintage one-liners, punctuated by his ever-present violin riffs and cries of "Take my wife – please!"

I wrote down some of the jokes he told that night so I could repeat them later to my friends and family. I couldn't write fast enough to keep pace with his delivery, but I did manage to get some of his act on paper, which I dutifully added to my expanding joke files.

So here, direct from my cache of stolen jokes, are some of the Youngman gems I scribbled down that magical night:

"A Jewish woman had two pet chickens. One got sick, so she killed the other one to make chicken soup for the sick one!"

"A bomb fell on Italy – and it slid off!"

"A newlywed couple was driving to Miami Beach and the groom put his hand on her knee. She said, 'We're married now, you can go a little further.' So he drove to Ft. Lauderdale!"

"A guy walked up to me and said, 'Do you see a cop around here?' I said, 'No.' He said, 'Stick 'em up!'"

"I told my mother-in-law, 'My house is your house.' Last week she sold it!"

"The traveling salesman asked the farmer to put him up for the night. The farmer said, 'Sure. But you'll have to sleep with my son.' 'Good Lord,' said the salesman, 'I'm in the wrong joke!'"

"My podiatrist told me he'd have me walking in no time. He did. He stole my car!"

I don't go on blind dates anymore. The last one I went on had bags OVER her eyes!"

"A panhandler said to me, 'Mister, I haven't tasted

food in a week.' I said, 'Don't worry, it still tastes the same!'"

"My doctor just gave me six months to live. I told him I couldn't pay his bill. So he gave me six more months!"

"Everyone in New York is so nasty. My uncle died there and he asked to be cremated – and have his ashes thrown in someone's face!"

"I asked a New Yorker how to get to Bellevue Hospital – and he broke my nose!

"I hate sushi. Why would I eat fish they use to catch other fish?"

"Last night, in this very room, they held the annual bulimia convention – the cake came out of the girl!"

"I just gave a donation to a halfway house – for girls who won't go all the way!"

"A guy held up a Chinese restaurant. He said, 'Give me all your money.' The owner said, 'To take out?'"

That night Henny told well over 100 jokes in rapid-fire succession. Some were funny, some corny, most were silly. It didn't matter if a joke was a clunker, another one followed immediately and eventually you'd hear one that made you roar with laughter. And there was plenty of laughter that night.

Henny Youngman was part of a great generation of comedians. Milton Berle, Shecky Green, Jerry Lewis, Sid Caesar, Red Buttons, Jan Murray (Dad), Sid Gould, Pat Cooper, Jack Carter, Norm Crosby, Alan King, Danny Thomas, Myron Cohen, Jackie Vernon, Phil Foster, Joey Bishop, Dick Shawn, Totie Fields, Redd Foxx, Phyllis Diller and so many others made America laugh for decades. Everyone knew their names and they enjoyed both fame and fortune. Sadly, the generations that adored them are dwindling down to a precious few, as are the comics they revered.

Henny Youngman, like all the rest, will be forgotten by future generations, but their jokes will be passed down and repeated forever. That's because you can't copyright a joke. Once it's told, it's public domain and we can repeat it forever.

Not everyone will laugh at the same jokes, of course. My father once said that if he told five people a joke, two would laugh, one wouldn't get it, one would say he heard it a different way, and one would say he could tell it better!

The thing about Youngman and all the others of that Golden Age of Comedy, was that their comedy, unlike today's so-called humor, didn't consist of shouting "F__k" for 45 minutes. Henny and the others knew that to make comedy ageless, the audience had to identify with the people, places, events and objects that they were talking about and find the funny side of those areas.

In their spirit, I've dedicated this book to them.

Take my jokes – please!

*At home with (from front to back) Buddy Hackett,
Phil Foster, Hal March, Sid Gould, Billy Vine,
Phil Silvers, Harvey Stone, Milton Berle,
Jan Murray (Dad) and Steve Allen*

ACKNOWLEDGEMENTS

Many thanks to Steve Schwab for his painstaking and time-consuming editing as well as for his insightful content input.

I'd also like to recognize the outstanding efforts put forth by award-winning artist Helane Freeman (ArtByHelane.com), who guided me through the unfamiliar world of book publishing. Her expertise simplified a process which for me was initially complicated, confusing and terrifying.

ABOUT THE AUTHOR

The oldest son of comedian and game show host Jan Murray, Warren Murray has taken his father's sage advice to always find the funny side of life.

Filled with true stories and personal recollections of growing up in the world of show business, you'll laugh out loud at the behind-the-scenes antics of the comedy legends who Warren was lucky to call his "uncles," including Milton Berle, Buddy Hackett, Jerry Lewis, Sid Caesar, Henny Youngman, Jack Carter, Don Rickles and so many others.

As a TV comedy writer/producer, and later as a network executive at NBC, Warren's tales from the golden age of TV provide a rarely-seen – and hilarious – look at the stars and showrunners from your favorite 70s and 80s sitcoms and game shows.

Also an award-winning educator, Warren gets an "A" for his brilliantly amusing and clever teaching methods that always kept his students on their toes. You'll wish Mr. Murray had been your middle school history teacher!

Warren also explores the funny side of everyday life, from growing up in 1950s Brooklyn with a soon-to-be-famous high school classmate to marriage, golf, religion, sex and old age.

Warren and his wife, Fran, happily reside in sunny California.

You can contact Warren with your comments, praise and condemnation at: warrensmurray@hotmail.com.

CPSIA information can be obtained
at www.ICGtesting.com
Printed in the USA
BVHW020041170721
612147BV00020B/1625